12 Steps to Unfold
Your Mediumistic Potential

Iris & Martin Magin

12 Steps
to Unfold Your
Mediumistic Potential

Bibliografische Information der Deutschen Nationalbibliothek:

Die Deutsche Nationalbibliothek verzeichnet diese Publikation in der Deutschen Nationalbibliografie; detaillierte bibliografische Daten sind im Internet über http://dnb.dnb.de abrufbar.

This book is based on the original German edition titled „12 Schritte zu deiner Medialität", written by Iris & Martin Magin and published in 2020. This English edition has been translated, updated and revised to adapt the content for an international audience.

Website: www.magin-impuls.de
Email: info@magin-impuls.de

Publisher: BoD · Books on Demand GmbH, In de Tarpen 42, 22848 Norderstedt, bod@bod.de
Print: Libri Plureos GmbH, Friedensallee 273, 22763 Hamburg

ISBN 978-3-7693-1824-1

Love units us

Contents

Chapter I: Introduction 3

Chapter II: Unfold Your Spirit Communication... 9

Facing Skepticism, Doubt and Fear _____ 10
Recognizing Spirit's True Voice_____ 13
The Journey of Spiritual Unfoldment _____ 15
Sacred Harmony: Nurturing Body, Mind and Spirit _____ 18
Exploring the Spectrum of Mediumship_____ 24

Chapter III: 12 Practice Steps to Unfold Your Mediumship 29

1. Exercise:Self-Awareness as the Foundation of Mediumship _____ 32
   Summary Exercise 1: Self-Awareness 35
2. Exercise: Unfolding Your Heart to the Power of Love _____ 36
   Summary Exercise 2: Unfolding Your Heart to the Power of Love........... 37
3. Exercise: Discovering Your Personal Spirit Guide _____ 38
   Summary Exercise 3: Discovering Your Personal Spirit Guide 40
4. Exercise: Strengthening your Mediumship through Self-Healing _ 42
   Summary Exercise 4: Strengthening your Mediumship 44
5. Exercise: lluminating Your Mind_____ 45
   Summary Exercise 5: Illuminating Your Mind: 46
6. Exercise: Experiencing the Magnitude of Your Own Soul_____ 47
   Summary Exercise 6: Experiencing the Magnitude of Your Own Soul: 49
7. Exercise: Emotional Growth as a Gateway to Mediumship _____ 50
   Summary Exercise 7: Emotional Growth 53
8. Exercise: Recognizing Different Spirit Guides _____ 53
   Summary Exercise 8: Recognizing Different Spirit Guides:.................... 58
9. Exercise: Connecting with Departed Loved Ones _____ 59
   Summary Exercise 9: Connecting with Departed Loved Ones 62
10. Exercise: Exploring Your Personal Mission _____ 63
    Summary Exercise 10: Exploring Your Personal Mission 64
11. Exercise: Strengthening Your Spirit Communication_____ 65
    Summary Exercise 11: Strengthen Your Communication 67
12. Exercise: Collecting your Mediumistic Benefits _____ 68
    Summary Exercise 12: Collecting your Mediumistic Benefits................ 70
    Taking Time to Rest on Your Mediumistic Journey_____ 71

Chapter IV: Shaping and Leading a Spiritual Practice Group *73*

Facilitating Growth as a Group Leader _____ 74
Foundational Principles for Mediumistic Collaboration: _____ 76
Crafting Your Practice Group's Purpose and Structure _____ 77
Welcoming Participants: Earthly and Spiritual _____ 79
Creating Your Ritual for Spiritual Connection_____ 81
Cultivating a Sacred Space for Spiritual Connection _____ 82
Designing Tailored Practice Exercises _____ 83
Facilitating Group Dynamics and Questions_____ 86
Facilitating Reflective Feedback_____ 87
Insights and Inspirations from Our Journey_____ 88

Chapter V: Frequently Asked Questions *90*

Chapter VI: Spirit Guide Teachings... *100*

Epilogue.. *109*

Attachments... *111*

Inspirational Reads: A Selection of Favorites _____ 113
The Language of Mediumship: Terms for Beginners _____ 115

Summary.. *121*

Acknowledgments... *122*

A Note to Attention

This book is not intended to and cannot replace any therapy or medical diagnosis. The authors neither directly nor indirectly give medical advice, nor do they prescribe the use of the "12 steps" as a form of treatment for illnesses without medical advice. You, the reader, will be shown ways to explore and develop your own mediumship.

Of course, you are entitled to use this information for self-treatment, but you should always consult a doctor or alternative practitioner if you experience any symptoms of illness. The advice in this book has been carefully compiled and checked by the authors; however, no guarantee can be given. Liability for any damage is excluded. Neither the authors nor the publisher can be held responsible for any consequences that may arise from the practical application or misuse of the information contained in this book. Anyone who carries out the techniques of the "12 Steps" for themselves without strictly following the instructions, explanations, and warnings of the authors does so solely at their own risk.

Chapter I:

Introduction

"Everyone dies, no one is dead"
(Tibetan Proverb)

The fear of dying and the uncertainty of what will happen when we are "dead" from a human perspective mean that our modern society is reluctant to consider this topic, let alone deal with it in any depth. The entertainment industry distracts us from everyday concerns with so-called 'fantastic ghosts', be they suspense, comedy, or drama. In other regions of the globe, however, death is handled in a completely conventional manner: the deceased relatives are held in high esteem, sought for guidance, and regularly communicated with. However, in the western world, mediums who contact the deceased tend to be personalities on the fringes of society. At best, they are ridiculed but often dismissed as cranks.

Anyone who wants to set out to acquire the appropriate "mediumistic translator skills" not only needs courage and steadfastness, but also the willingness to step out of the social fabric (for a while). Occasionally, you need to pay more attention to your own inner voice than to the opinions and views of others.

The love for people and love between people are the characteristics of a medium's work in this world. This is how communication is born. The medium acts like a kind of telephone. It is the bearer of the message and nothing more, but also nothing less. The more clearly the medium can establish a connection with souls from another life as a telephone, the clearer and more memorable and touching the communication that takes place, for both sides.

*

3

Before we continue, we would like to take this moment to briefly introduce ourselves, as it is not the author who is writing this book on her own, but she is doing so in partnership with us, spiritual beings from another life. Some readers may be surprised here because it sounds so strange to the ears of this material world that the inspiration for this book comes from higher forces and not just from the author herself. We have been working with Iris Magin for a very long time —some of us since her conception. We, a team of spiritual helpers, have taken on the task of strengthening the connection between the worlds and training "mediumistic interpreters" who enable communication across time and space. Much of this does not stem from Iris's experience and expertise alone, but is based on a wide range of observations, experiences, and a comprehensive understanding on our part. This is also a new, unfamiliar way of working together for the author, and this book is both dictated to Iris by us and supplemented by personal experiences of both Martin and Iris. Our contributions are marked with standard type, whereas those of Iris or her husband Martin are marked with *italics*.

In the following, we will also refer to the worldly ambassadors as "mediums." We call the recipients of our delivered messages, blessings, and healing energies "recipients" and the deceased, souls or beings from the other life, "spiritual beings", "spirit guides "or "spirit friends".

*

You as human beings frequently solely focus on the mediumistic effects on your side. But how much delight and joy you create on our side because here too there is a longing to connect and bridge what seems so unbridgeable in the spirit on earth. The tasks of the mediumistic "telephone" are manifold. You begin with a clear intention and willingness to be "called" and to maintain the connection as a neutral medium. Furthermore, as a medium, you develop the trust that someone will call, even if it sometimes happens that a recipient waits in vain for a call from the spirit world. Furthermore, it is important to disregard your own personal aspects, inclinations, and preferences as far as possible. You stay as close as possible to what is being conveyed, as if you are a good translator of languages. You are mainly translating from one "language" to the respective other "language".

We perceive your messages in the form of sounds and bright colors, and less through words or emotional sensations. You, in turn, often perceive the connection through physical or emotional sensations and measure the quality of a transmission by this. As a medium, you will take yourself out of the game, but at the same time you need to be present. You step into the background and yet, you are the central link, just like a simultaneous translator. Your own emotions, opinions, and interpretations are undesirable, as they can change the tone and character of the message or even distort it (usually unintentionally).

To take over the role of an "uncommitted mediumistic telephone", you as a medium must first get to know and accept yourself well. If you are unfamiliar with your own biases, fixed ideas, values, and emotional sensitivities, it will be difficult for you to behave in a new way, i.e. not to become creative on your own authority. It is as if you, as the medium, are temporarily relinquishing your own self, the persona, to assume and convey the character traits, language habits, and emotions of another being as an intermediary.

This is particularly the case in the context of contact with the deceased. In the field of philosophical speech, the character of the spiritual being becomes apparent through the metaphors used, choice of words and its unique reactions. And in the healing discipline, you as the medium become a channel for the healing energies that flow to the recipient. The less the medium's own person stands in the way, the more intensively the energy can flow. This is why this role is often referred to as being a "pure channel".

It is characterized by the fact that the medium knows himself well and withdraws as a person while working as a medium. Carried by a selfless love, the medium experiences boundless joy in conveying the messages.

There are some mediums who can withdraw themselves much more easily than others and allow us divine beings to enter. At the beginning of their mediumistic development journey, many beginners are heavily dependent on their own human intuition. They do not yet let us spiritual helpers really connect with them deeply. However, this form of mediumship is predominantly based on personal intuitive abilities and less on the solutions "conjured up" by us spiritual entities.

We therefore roughly divide mediums into those who intuitively "read" others and mediums who predominantly convey messages in connection with us. At best, the former are inspired by us. The latter, on the other hand, are mirrored by us in their nature during the transmission of the message so that they can take on character traits from us in their communication.

*

In this book, we will provide you with a mediumistic toolbox/ packed rucksack based on our current knowledge, which will make it easier for you both to get started and to make progress on your mediumistic path. We aim to accompany you on your psychic journey and to provide you with our experience, knowledge, and skills as a tour guide. Get ready to embark on a journey that will not only allow you to experience the ups and downs of life intensively and calmly, but that will also enable you, from a certain point on your personal journey, to act independently and confidently as a psychic mediator between the worlds.

In this first chapter of the book, you will be given a brief introduction to the nature and meaningfulness of communicating with deceased loved ones. Building on this, the second chapter presents the personal and organizational requirements that serve as the basis for a successful mediumistic journey. From the third chapter onwards, we will introduce you to the individual learning steps of the mediumistic journey, offer a great deal of practical relevance, and introduce you to the possible worlds of mediumistic experience through personal experiences and case studies. In the fifth chapter, we present the questions that often arise during such a challenging mediumistic journey and give you, our answers. As with everything that is written in this book, this reflects the truth that is valid at the moment of publication. However, like everything in this world, this truth is subordinate to the living power of creation and can change, expand, and dissolve.

Iris 24: This self-study book on developing personal mediumship was originally written by me, Iris, in 2018. Each morning, I dedicated 20 minutes over the course of about six weeks to practicing the art of trance writing, during which this text emerged. At the time, I never seriously considered publishing it; I felt awed and humbled by the renowned mediums and teachers we had encountered. here were already so many insightful books on the market that I wondered, why should I add mine?

In September 2019, my husband Martin and I received the remarkable gift of direct communication with "Rudolph," a beloved spirit friend, while Martin in a sleeping and deeper trance state. "Rudolph" is a borrowed human personality channeled by what is referred to us as the "All-Oneness." Since then, he has communicated with us regularly during trance sessions, providing inspirational insights and spiritual teachings.

In 2020, "Rudolph" encouraged us to publish this book online in German, which we successfully did. To our surprise, about six weeks ago in October 2024, "Rudolph" asked us that we translate the German version into English using artificial intelligence.

This request was extraordinary, as "Rudolph" rarely asks us for anything. We honored his wish and began the translation process. However, as we translated the text into English, we noticed that our perspectives on certain parts of the book had evolved over the past six years.

As a result, while we aimed to stay as true as possible to the original German version, we occasionally incorporated new insights, experiences, and perspectives we've gained since its initial publication. These additions are marked with a "24" label at the beginning of each relevant paragraph.

We are profoundly grateful for this opportunity to reflect on how much we have grown since publishing the first German edition in 2020. We hope that one day you, too, will have the chance to enjoy your mediumistic experiences and recognize how far you have come on your own mediumistic journey.

With love,

Iris and Martin

Chapter II:

Unfold Your Spirit Communication

Love is the essence that makes it possible to communicate with each other between worlds. It is the love of a father for his son that makes it possible for both to encounter each other and to seek it. It is the dead daughter, who died too soon, who wants to dock onto with the longing of the mother left behind. And it is love and the willingness to serve a higher power and force that enables the meeting of two souls who miss each other deeply. The power of love is like a current: the stronger it flows, the easier and clearer the connection becomes. Love does not allow itself to be distracted by resistance but enables an inner clarity that what is happening is right and true. It is thanks to your love that you have this book in front of you today, and your love will guide you forward step by step until you experience for yourself that nothing can separate you from living your love. Thus, love is the core, the foundation, and the bond of mediumistic work. Nothing equals it, and every good medium is carried in their work by this eternal force of unconditional love.

Trust in what we call the power of creation, and what you call God, is also the foundation that makes good communication possible. This trust can be renewed step by step: it is an aspect of mediumistic training, but it does not belong only in practice rooms. No, this trust in the divine is often strengthened and purified through events in daily life. Having trust means being at peace and having the courage to embrace the unknown. It means not allowing yourself to be influenced by personal doubts, fears, feelings of inferiority, or false comparisons with others. It is an inner calm and centeredness that ensures you do no longer resonate with the fears of the recipient but, instead, can transform the emotions you encounter with your own stillness, serenity, and centeredness. To have trust in the divine elemental power, to increase and strengthen this trust is the fundamental task of every mediumistic journey. The quality and conciseness of the connection to us depends largely on this trust.

Facing Skepticism, Doubt and Fear

How does one move forward in this life with so many material constraints? How to become a medium when the world around seems so dark, so lost, and so chaotic? These perceptions are valid, as they highlight that the work is more necessary than ever. For the fear of death exists in this world like a rapidly spreading virus. So, the belief that everything ends with death also leads to less responsibility being taken for one's own life than would be necessary from our perspective. It is not the world that is dark, but what people have made of it, and that also means that you are part of it and play your part in it.

This leads us to another component that represents a significant challenge for the medium: handling one's own fear. The fear of speaking out, and the fear that what comes through will make no sense or will not receive the desired positive response, is a factor that causes many mediumistic freshmen to stumble. Their own doubts, fear of failure, and frustration about the poor results cause many to quit at a point when they need not. Thus, the journey is not a journey to happiness in the short term, but a journey that leads to a short —term confrontation with one's own concepts of perception and limitations of fear and skepticism.

M: In the fall of 2011, the Scottish medium Gordon Smith once again came to Frankfurt/Main, invited by the Frankfurter Ring e.V.. Iris wanted to experience Gordon live and persuaded me to join her at an evening event with the probably best-known and most intensively researched British Scottish medium at that time. With great skepticism, I agreed, aware that Iris had seen Gordon multiple times before and had only good experiences to share. But the evening was a big, big disappointment for me. I felt as if I were in a theater or magic show. Gordon Smith worked from the lower edge of the stage in the large hall of the "Haus der Jugend", a youth hostel in Frankfurt. He spoke of being in contact with the deceased and delivered messages from the deceased to recipients sitting in the hall. My inner skepticism prevented me from feeling the positive energies of the evening. Instead, everything I saw and heard in the evening made me dismiss it as mere "charade."

Nevertheless, my curiosity persisted. Though I couldn't trust this "performance," I wanted to know how "this" worked. As experienced volunteers of the Frankfurter Ring, we became course administrators for Gordon Smith and Steven Levett, and my journey toward developing my own mediumistic abilities began to unfold unrelentingly.

The first of four weekends took place shortly after my initial encounter with Gordon. I arrived at the venue alongside Iris with a rather unusual level of nervousness for me — after all, I had been working as a volunteer at Frankfurter Ring e.V. for almost 12 years and with many teachers meanwhile. "Coincidentally," we were an odd number of participants that day. Gordon began the workshop with a guided meditation. To my surprise, tears streamed down my cheeks during the meditation. I let this exercise move and touch me in a way I hadn't experienced in a long time. Now I was genuinely surprised and stunned. Who was this man, this medium, and what was happening to me?

Without pause, Gordon continued: he arranged the 41 participants in inner and outer circles and had them practice in pairs. I was still carrying my skepticism, I breathed a deep sigh of relief, thinking I could sit out the exercise since I had no partner. But I was wrong. When Gordon saw, I was trying to opt out of the exercise, he came over, sat opposite to me, and asked me to give him a reading of the deceased. So, there I was—a skeptic and novice— facing the renowned medium Gordon Smith. I had no time to reject because Steven Levett, Gordon's protégé and friend, had already begun explaining the exercise. So, in the truest sense of the word: eyes closed and through! I gathered my courage, looked into Gordon's blue eyes, and began to speak. I mentioned hills, the number seven, passing clouds, and more. Gordon nodded kindly and, in his feedback, even confirmed that he could relate to the images I had seen and described. He related my descriptions to one of his upcoming trips. Yet, at that moment, I couldn't accept his positive feedback because, from my perspective, my statements felt far too trivial...

Mediumistic perception and therefore the quality of the messages is strongly determined by your own spiritual maturity. Here too, the medium is prepared to master the difficult tests of being questioned and having to explain themselves to third parties who are used to approaching topics with skepticism and everyday ignorance. It also leads mediums tending to want to satisfy the expectations of their recipients —after all, it gives them a little sense of power and grandeur to fulfill the longings of the bereaved. An untrained medium may not realize when they are communicating with us from an authentic connection and when they are crossing over into the land of their own fantasies. A receiver can recognize this very well if they are alert. In this way, skepticism, doubt and rational questioning on the part of the recipient help the learning medium to avoid getting lost in their own worlds and wishful narratives.

So, we encourage you, dear readers, to adopt one of the practical exercises in your life from now on: to learn a constructive approach to your own fears and the fears of others. This is achieved through mediumistic exercises that are offered to you as part of life lessons, and it is your choice whether to embrace these lessons and develop yourself through them. Like a good immune system, fears, doubts, and your own skepticism are the forces that make you more resilient in dealing with the mediumistic "storms".

Recognizing Spirit's True Voice

Everything that happens can and should be questioned, and indeed, must be doubted at the beginning. After all, our imagination is strong enough to produce phenomena that nobody would normally consider possible. Imagination, the power of visualization, is the essence with which we work. Yet, it also has its own dynamics. You, as a medium, are in a good position if you learn to recognize and control this very individual dynamic of your own imagination. It is not the words themselves that provide proof of the other world. Rather, it is the loving energies and other factors that do not fit into the usual perceptual framework.

A recipient of mediumistic messages has the means to verify or develop a sense of trust to be able to determine whether the messages really come from a spiritual source. Often, in a strong, intense connection with the spirit world, an altered perception is one of the key signs. This perception can manifest as a pleasant feeling of peace, self-assurance, or love. In numerous instances, even a little information triggers strong emotional reactions, and many mediums feel that they feel different as a person than they did in the moment before the reading. Sensations such as a cool shiver, a slight tingling sensation, as if a pleasant current is spreading, are also possible. Others see a light or specific colors and recognize in this way that a message is not of worldly origin.

A second way to verify the desired message's validity is through exploration. The recipient inwardly asks questions to the spirit world before or during the reading and then waits to see if these questions are answered. If they are answered *(I: I have experienced that this ideally happens almost simultaneously)*, the recipient can probably assume that the connection is genuine and exists in all its goodness.

The third alternative is that the message conveys topics that only the recipient can understand and no one else can: whether it's an apple tree that was planted together when the deceased was young or a motorcycle accident that has never been spoken of. Whatever the proof is that only oneself can know, as soon as these private details are conveyed by the medium, the recipient's trust rapidly increases.

*

M: ...but suddenly, Gordon grew excited and said to me: "Yes, but Martin, I do have a message for you!" And immediately, Gordon began giving me a reading from the deceased. Gordon spoke of an older man who observed me sitting at my work in front of a series of numbers and photographs. This old man sensed my desperation in the face of these complex lists of numbers and pictures. And he encouraged me to finally take the next step and put the numbers and pictures together. This older man later revealed himself in the reading as my paternal grandfather. He appeared with his shortened leg, his oversized orthopedic shoe, his hand missing a thumb, and his caring side, which extended not only to his own large family but also to strangers and those in need; my grandfather managed the family business, a bakery, and pastry shop.

At that time, I was indeed struggling with a major book project, which I hadn't told in my immediate circle about it. At that time, I did not dare to compile the catalog raisonné of works of a German animal sculptor. The task of matching historical photographs of animal sculptures with a series of data —such as time of creation, materials, and technique used, size, location, edition numbers, and so on, all the information recorded in columns— was too much for me. I simply lacked the confidence to make critical art historical decisions. As so often, I was just afraid of the potential success of my work. Consequently, I simply left this project untouched until then.

However, Gordon's reading of the deceased grandfather struck me like a small earthquake. Gordon knew NOTHING about me at that time. And here he brought me my deceased grandfather, who had seen me lately as I sat in despair and fear of doing something wrong, doing nothing whatsoever.

In a nutshell: This reading from the deceased gave me the necessary push to write the artist's catalog raisonné. I took a week off, rented a room in a remote hotel, assigned the numbers, data, and facts to the images, and began to write the texts with determination. Fifteen months later, I held the completed catalog, fresh from the press, sent from the publisher, in my hands. My thanks still go to Gordon and to my dear grandfather!

You as the medium can expect that the recipient's trust in you as a medium is not or will not remain stable after a mediumistic sitting. For this reason, the recipient will also repeatedly seek a conversation with us, the spirit world, approaching different mediumistic personalities until their own trust has been sustainably strengthened. For the skeptical recipient, a critical engagement with a very unusual and, for most, strange situation means that the initial fear does not grow any further. On the contrary, the recipient's own open-mindedness unfolds and ultimately culminates in a state of trust and love. For your own development as a medium it is important to experience this skepticism and inner resistance of the recipient. This will strengthen your own trust into the spirit world and thus increases the perceived clarity of the connection between you, as a medium and us, spirit guides.

The Journey of Spiritual Unfoldment

In this way, you as the medium will grow over time both in terms of your mediumistic abilities (the development of which is the focus of this book) and in terms of your spiritual personality. The mediumistic abilities learned on earth also help the deceased soul in the spirit world side to grasp and resolve the lessons collected on earth more quickly. Without being able to estimate the final effect, each one of you who embarks on the mediumistic path facilitates the work of so many other souls, both in your earthly and in our spiritual world.

This is also why it is so important to us to support mediums in their development, regardless of age. Everything learned here on earth —even if only briefly before transitioning to the other life— can later serve us in the ongoing unfolding of divine potential. History shows that many well-known mediums in England practiced their mediumistic abilities once they were of advanced age. The threads that bind souls to the earth grow thinner in older age, making people more receptive to our words. However, this does not mean that age is a prerequisite for working successfully as a medium.

Many who practice mediumship today and, in the past, have had these abilities since birth. Just as other people have talents that later allow them to become virtuoso pianists, singers, or successful chess champions. Others open themselves up to the mediumistic discipline during their lives if they have created the spiritual prerequisites for these very sacred gifts to be made available to them through skill and/or their own aspirations. Here too, there are many different starting points from which you can begin. But they all point in the same direction: to make themselves available to others in love and peace to serve as healing messengers in both worlds. Thus, respect for one's own greatness and the greatness of all those involved in communication is one of the signs by which we recognize how much a medium's personality has grown.

M: I believe that we all have mediumistic abilities within us from birth; however, we have lost access to them and can now rediscover them through intensive exercises. Looking back, I recall several events in my early childhood that make me believe today that we are born as mediumistic beings (and beyond that).

At around eight years old, as I lay in my bed falling asleep, I felt my astral body detach from my physical body and slowly levitate toward the ceiling. I observed myself in complete darkness from two perspectives: once lying in bed, looking up through my closed eyes, and once looking down from the ceiling. Without worry or fear, I watched from both perspectives simultaneously, perceiving and allowing. When I told my mother about it the next morning, I received only a sympathetic glance and the question whether I had eaten too much the night before. Thereafter, I forgot about the incident.

Another time, in the middle of the night, I felt hands on my eyelids. Fingertips reached for my eyelids and through the lids towards my irises. I felt as if the iris, as if the irides were being pulled away from the eyeballs. The panic that initially flared up died away when I engaged in a conversation with a spiritual being, who told me in a few words: "It's not your eyes you're seeing with!"

A few years later, I would frequently sleepwalk through my room and the adjoining rooms in my parents' house. While sleepwalking, that is, with my eyes closed, I could "see" precisely where each piece of furniture stood, which doors were open, and which ones were closed and needed opening. After completing my rounds, I would return to bed. Only once was I startled out of my sleepwalking by a loud, disorienting sound that only I could hear; I stumbled, tripped, and hit my forehead against the edge of a table. That noise woke my parents, who rushed me to the village doctor; a small scar above my right eye still bears the mark of this accident. My nighttime walks ended with this event.

These are the events that happened to me in my youth, which I can remember today thanks to years of meditation. Today, I interpret them as attempts by the spirit world to establish contact with me and offer evidence of their existence, in a way that now feels strange to me, but perhaps it was the only way I could understand back then. So, the spirit world chose an approach that I could perceive.

I: When I began my training with Gordon Smith in 2013, I was convinced that I had no innate mediumistic gift and that I was essentially starting from scratch. I could neither see auras nor perceive the deceased; I had not experienced any enduring, consciousness —expanding states. My basic scientific training as a psychologist had steered me in a

direction that was contrary to everything, I experienced later in my me-
diumistic training. Today, I realize that my life path and challenging life
events prepared me to be at least open to the topic of "communication
with the deceased" and trance. I now believe that, as an ordinary per-
son, I did acquire my mediumistic gifts later in life, thanks to the help of
excellent teachers and with discipline and great joy.

I 24: With the appearance of "Rudolph" in our lives, I gradually realized
that my previous life path had thoroughly prepared me for the role I
play when Martin works as a "sleeping trance medium." At the time of
our first encounter, I was a professional expert in leadership assess-
ments and development. Over more than 20 years, I had conducted nu-
merous high-stakes assessments to identify the right executives for open
positions. This experience trained me to ask probing and clarifying
questions, adapt to others' spontaneous needs, and remain calm when
facing emotionally challenging interview partners. Transitioning into
the role of interview partner and group facilitator in dialogue with our
spirit friend "Rudolph" felt like a natural progression in my develop-
ment.

Sacred Harmony: Nurturing Body, Mind and Spirit

Do not let yourself influence by aggressive or depressive humans,
by hopelessness, sorrow, and the lack of willingness to show understanding. When you learn to let got your attachment of what
happens on the outside, trust will grow in yourself and to your
spirit guides.

Here we can use our knowledge to accompany people who are
ready to accept this special secret and mystery. Because ultimately the same applies here: only the willingness and ability to
understand others more deeply allow love and compassion to
spread further within you as the medium. This understanding
cannot be gained solely on earth, for human ability alone is not
enough to penetrate matters to their core, and you as the medium

will often fall short in interpreting your own perceptions and judgments. Therefore, we recommend that you study not only ancient scriptures and the works of wise or mediumistic personalities, but also to continue developing disciplines of the heart and building physical strength.

The latter is often neglected by mediums. Here we would like to ask you to look after the temple and the vessel you are using carefully and promote it in your own way. Do not rest too much after performing mediumistic work; instead, take a short walk, move your cells so that they may keep you going for a long time.

You may ask yourself: "What happens in my body during mediumistic work?" You will come to notice, like with any other work, there will be days when you feel lighter, happier, and more agile after mediumistic work. And there will be other days when you feel the heaviness, sluggishness, and vulnerability of your body. Both states are valid and, like any other work, are part of your daily life. Do not overinterpret one or the other and let neither tendency divert you from your path. This is a necessary pendulum movement of the body to cope with the new experiences of your personality.

M 24: The transition to becoming a trance medium was as surprising as it was unplanned. This made it even more important for me to define my personal position and, above all, to clarify what I wanted to achieve as an individual, whom I wanted to serve, and most importantly: what I did NOT want to do.

The numerous trainings and courses I had the privilege of attending — particularly in mediumistic and spiritual disciplines— provided a solid foundation and connected me with a wide range of teachers. I had the opportunity to get to know these teachers not only on stage but also in informal moments before and after events, as well as in private settings. With some, I realized their stage presence was almost theatrical, while their private demeanor was entirely different. Like many others, I also witnessed how vulnerable some mediums could be during a trance session, how much protection they needed, and, most notably, the consequences when that protection was lacking. I also observed how physically exhausted many mediums appeared immediately after a session. With these insights in mind, it became crucial for me to establish an agreement with my friends from the spirit world:

> "I will emerge from my full trance sessions feeling neutral or even strengthened, and under no circumstances physically depleted. "

This agreement has guided my work as a trance medium ever since. It provides me with confidence and freedom to connect with the spirit world and step fully into my role as a facilitator. It allows me to embrace this role as a mediator with a sense of freedom and deeper trust, enabling me to serve as a clear and open channel for communication between worlds.

Naturally, internal tension accompanied my initial sessions. Nervousness and curiosity often took center stage, leading to physical discomforts like dizziness, headaches, and muscle tightness afterwards. However, with the above agreement in place, these sensations quickly subsided and have not returned to this day. On the contrary, I sometimes come out of sessions feeling revitalized, and even symptoms like previous colds, headaches, or pain in my knee have occasionally disappeared during the trance process.

A key strength in my practice is my partnership with Iris. She is by my side during every trance session, holding the space and serving as my greatest source of support. Without her, I would not engage in my trance work. Imagine this: You fall asleep, wake up, and discover that you've been speaking for some time —perhaps even inspiring others— but you have no memory of what you said. Your only awareness is the sensation of having enjoyed a deep, restful sleep. Yet, you remain fully (and legally) responsible for everything you said while in a full-trance state. The lack of control over what was said leaves you questioning your boundaries, wondering where "you" ends and the "spirit world" begins. There's a fragility at that moment, an awareness of just how exposed you are when trust is the only bridge between you and the divine.

*Looking back, there were moments when I was startled out of trance —
for various reasons— but Iris reassuring words, "It's all okay, Martin.
Just return to your trance state. I'm right here with you," helped me in
those rare instances. Iris presence allowed me to move on without
giving those moments any undue significance.*

At this point, we also want to emphasize that vulnerability, in our
sense, does not exist. What you are made of is invulnerable and
cannot be destroyed. Sensitive perceptions naturally make you
more open to the spectrum of all possible perceptions, allowing
you to experience aspects of life for the first time, perhaps more
intensely and clearly, sometimes to the point of an almost unbear-
able intensity of being.

This, too, is merely a phenomenon, and it is essential not to focus
too much on it. Just as a permeable garment exposes the skin to
more wind, rain, or sunshine, you will gradually allow the diversity of life to come closer to you. However, know that in these
moments, you possess everything you need to cope with new
conditions. Because that is also what this is about: consciously
deciding to recognize and appreciate who you are with all your
creative power and your diverse potentials, and to trust these
new abilities. In moments when you are challenged by your supposed hypersensitivity, you can demonstrate that you possess
both skills: to deal with it effectively and the trust in yourself and
in us, your spirit friends, that nothing harmful will happen to you
and others.

The attachment to emotional sensitivity may serve as a good compass in your relationships with others at the beginning of your
mediumistic path, but it should not be the Grail (Parzival legend
= Holy Chalice) that leads you to the joy of being. In this context,
the Grail is simply the trust in your own strength, in your mediumistic abilities, and above all, in your love. It cannot be shaken
by anything apart from your own self —doubting and destructive
thoughts.

The body is less vulnerable than you think, and though this is not our focus today, let us just say this: The body should be "worn" like a good garment. You care for this garment respectfully, but you do not see yourself as the garment. Instead, you identify with what fills the garment. In the same way, get to know your body well, respect it, and protect it as needed. But be aware: you are not this piece of divine clothing because as soon as it has done its job, it is laid aside, and you move on in your non-material form.

The life of a medium does not change in the way newcomers often perceive or wish to perceive. For, before you already embarked on your path to mediumship, one, or the other of your inner organs of perception has already developed. Only then does one become interested in embarking on the path of mediumship. Moreover, the love to serve is present at the beginning of your mediumistic journey, and this service may then continue to grow.

The life of a medium changes only to the extent that the future medium devotes more time and space to this area of interest, thereby facing the task of reassessing time management and priorities in one's life. This is often overlooked at the beginning of the mediumistic journey because, as with learning any new skill or engaging in a new hobby, this also means that, for a time that the previous priorities may have to be abandoned for a while.

The medium also quickly learns that a deeper desire to gain the special recognition of others is not fulfilled in this way. On the contrary, many who embark on this journey will discover that others pay little attention or show little interest in this new passion. This is justified. After all, this is where the gift of pursuing something unconditionally, without recognition, is practiced.

The joy and love in the act are the only rewards to be collected at the beginning. Over time, even a sense of detachment arises: in one moment, you are actively engaged as a medium with your gift, and in the next moment, you are back in your ordinary state of being. Everything feels very neutral and harmonious, with no great sense of pride or satisfaction. After all, they expect the state of inner contentment, the feeling of connectedness, and the sense of this special, sacred moment to continue after the session.

But this is not the case. This is where the dangers lie that have already led people in ancient cultures not to share the path to mediumship with the public: the danger of becoming addicted to a state of consciousness that is not one's own but is only borrowed for the moment of exercising the gift. A selfish, unloving and possibly poorly prepared mediumistic work amplifies fear of mediumistic abilities, fuels superstition, and does not serve the greater good.

You may wonder, "Can I not feel satisfaction, joy, and pride after a successful session? "And we tell you: Yes, you can, and especially at the beginning, this will help you to maintain your motivation to practice the art with discipline. But the moment will come when you slip into a feeling of "That was it, and it was good"; you will concentrate on what lies ahead of you and retain few memories and thoughts of what lies behind you.

The love and connection in the moment of mediumistic work are the rewards you collect. They are more profound than you can imagine in your human existence. The love and respect of those who work with you from our world, and sometimes from the earthly side as well, will accompany you and be as comprehensive and constant as you rarely experience on earth. This is what we wish to share with you at the beginning, and this explanation may help as you encounter similar practice states and experiences.

Exploring the Spectrum of Mediumship

We differentiate countless mediumistic channels as well as countless degrees in the practice of mediumship. In your *(European)* cultural sphere, clairsentience (feeling, sensing), clairvoyance (seeing), and clairaudience (hearing) are especially well known, as are telepathy and intuitive knowing. Beyond these, there are also forms of clairalience (smelling) and clairgustance (tasting) defined. These are all mediumistic channels that you can explore and experience in more detail in the upcoming exercises.

M: Once, I observed how mediumistic clairvoyance is not widely accepted in public spaces when I was sitting in a subway. I overheard a little girl, perhaps six years old, asking her parents: "Why are they under the ceiling? Can't they get out of here?" The parents remained silent, obviously feeling that their child's question was inappropriate and embarrassing. I, however, looked with interest in the direction of the subway car ceiling and sensed energies, still faint, yet I could feel that there was something there.

These channels can be used for various mediumistic disciplines, all of which have one purpose in common: to prove and make it possible to experience that there is more than just this world in which you live. And that your soul will collect even more experiences in the so-called afterlife. They can provide you with access to support that can make your life easier, more peaceful, and more harmonious. So, all disciplines are ultimately healing in one way or another.

In mediumistic communication, you as the medium have the opportunity to access information on a horizontal, personal level or on a vertical spiritual level. On a horizontal level, your intention is to "read the sitter" in front of you, in the sense of psychic or intuitive reading, capturing events or experiences from the life of the recipient or by using surrogates of deceased individuals. This art can be learned through diligence. It results in expanding your mediumistic perception on a horizontal level between those involved, supporting you in your vertical mediumistic work.

Additionally, there are the disciplines of vertical mediumistic transmission, in which a spiritual helper from our side is heavily involved. We distinguish afterlife communication or communication with the deceased from the transmission of messages (channeling) and mediumistic healing, which we make tangible later in our exercises.

*

The first discipline we would like to introduce is one that focuses on afterlife contacts or communication with the deceased. The contact with beloved deceased beings is established through a medium on your side and a medium (also called "spirit helper, friend or guide") on our side. This ability is a very sacred gift and requires a great deal of inner strength, personal maturity and courage, especially since this mediumistic discipline is still met with significant skepticism and resistance in your culture.

The second discipline is often called "channeling" in German-speaking countries (may referred to as "philosophical communication" in England) and includes the transmission of messages to a sitter. The content extends from the mere communication of more or less personal to philosophical messages to the recipient. Channeling is less about identifying or recognizing a specific deceased person.

Here, the boundary between what the medium says to another person and a genuine communication between our spirit world and yours is most fragile. This type of mediumistic communication can cause unsightly deviations and misinterpretations. For here, too, the healing quality of the message depends on how far the medium sets aside their interests, desires, and needs to fully serve and devote themselves to bringing messages from our spirit world to yours. This is where the quality criteria that we have already mentioned in earlier chapters come into play as an important differentiating criterion.

There is also the possibility of connecting with us, spiritual beings, for the purpose of healing oneself and others. There are numerous variations of mediumistic healing forms. What they all have in common is that the degree or intensity of the connection between the medium and us spiritual beings is a critical factor for success.

I: On our mediumistic development journey, we personally encountered spirit healers such as João de Deus, Jesus Lopez, Rade Maric as well-known mediums, such as Gordon Smith, Steven Levett, Eileen Davis, Nicole Jansen, Mikel Lizerralde, Scott Milligan, Matthew Smith, or John Upton, in deeper or even full trance states. In full trance, it becomes evident to those present that the medium's own personality steps aside in favor of an overlay by another spiritual entity. Clairsentient individuals may also feel a shift in the room's atmosphere density, and clairvoyant individuals may perceive colors or, in some cases, see the spirit helpers in their full form while working through the medium.

I 24: Since "Rudolph" appeared as a spiritual family member to us, I have learned to recognize changes in energy before, during, and after our trance sessions. "Rudolph" also creates experiences that build and deepen our trust in our mutual connection.

Without initially knowing how "Rudolph" might have looked during his earthly life, I consistently envisioned a strong inner image of him in his later years. Soon, we discovered one of his pictures on the internet, and it closely matched the image I had perceived internally while in dialogue with him.

Occasionally, "Rudolph" also makes subtle noises, such as creaks, or manifests physical phenomena. Early on, I received a unique physical sign during a session with "Rudolph": A scar appeared on Martin's cheek. And once he talked in an unknown language to us. We later discovered that he had spoken to us in Aramaic. These are just a few examples of how our spirit friend nurtured our trust in him as a guide by providing us with such wonderful experiences.

The degree of connection between the medium and our world can vary greatly depending on the medium's developmental current state. Some mediums, upon reaching advanced stages of development, enter a full trance, where they partially or even entirely lose awareness of what is being communicated through their voice. They enter a dream- or sleep-like state. Early on we were taught, that this state is challenging to achieve, and only a few manage to develop this gift or the motivation and dedication for it on their mediumistic journey.

I 24: Today, we know from our own experience with "Rudolph", that if the spirit world chooses you as a sleeping trance medium, as it is the case with Martin, they will do so independently from your own personal or spiritual development's efforts.

We, from the beyond, use every degree of receptivity of you as an earthly medium in our work. We begin with the inspirational work within the framework of your everyday awareness, then proceed to actively shaping experiences of mutual mediumistic connection as well as bonding and continue to deeper states of relaxation or trance. To increase your own mediumistic sensitivity and receptiveness, from our perspective, the state, and active or passive cooperation of you as a medium matter less than your capacity for love and devotion.

Chapter III:

12 Practice Steps to Unfold Your Mediumship

If you have decided to follow the mediumistic path, the question often arises: What is the best way to proceed? Well, in addition to the exercise sequences suggested below, it is recommended that you also try to develop your own mediumship in joint training and exercise groups. From our perspective, the choice of worldly teachers on mediumship and the specific themes covered in online or in-person training as well as private practice groups should fit to your own preferred learning style.

However, as you will come to realize, your true teachers are not of this earthly world but reside in the spiritual realm. They will guide you toward your next learning adventure. For this reason, your focus should extend beyond attending mediumistic training classes or private practice circles. To truly learn how to be guided directly by your personal spirit teachers from the other side, we ask for one thing above all: your time and discipline.

Time is needed for your personal practice sequences, your own personal growth, and to create the awareness space to let yourself be guided directly by your spirit teachers. Discipline, in the sense of commitment and perseverance to overcome difficult times of development. Even when you are learning to swim, you have phases in which not everything goes smoothly, your motivation wanes and doubt sets in. This is also the case when learning the gifts of mediumship. Regular practice helps to consolidate what you have learned. It also provides those from the spirit world with a steady framework to connect.

The human body in particular can learn and develop much better in a rhythmically structured environment than under irregular space and time conditions. However, this is also only one recommended aid to strengthen your discipline for practicing. The paths to exploring your own mediumistic skills can entail that you practice spontaneously over and over again without having to commit to fixed time schedules.

I: My professional work as a business consultant, with its varied travel schedules, work hours, and overnight situations, seemed like a disruptive obstacle to my disciplined practice, especially at the beginning. Yet, I quickly learned that, as long as I showed a serious intention, practice was possible at any time and place. In places that I initially found difficult to practice in silence, the initial feeling of disturbance —thanks to my friends from the spirit world— was no longer present after a few minutes. This taught me that my own thoughts and perceptions ("this place is too noisy to practice") could inhibit my own discipline of practicing my own mediumship. At any time, my spirit guides could work closely with me if I wanted to or if the situation required it.

Fear may arise of not doing it right or well enough when practicing by yourself. This can hinder your discipline and your time investment. When confronted with your fear, there is only one effective strategy: Recognize or accept that you are afraid. Take a decision to go into trust and follow love instead. You can always ask us, your spirit guides, for support and assistance. Everything you really need to enhance your mediumship is available! Try it out, even in your everyday life. You will see that it will work wonderfully after initial difficulties. When practicing, it is important to follow your inner impulses —whether they are a thought, a feeling, or perhaps also an inner desire. Love, light, and your willingness to serve others with a wonderful gift are what guide you, and nothing else.

If doubting thoughts or fears arise, we ask you to tell yourselves inwardly: "I trust my higher self and all the creative, radiant, and positive forces that accompany me on this path." And if you know other ways of being mindful and appreciating your own experience and being, take the path that is familiar to you, as this will lead you to the desired goal with joy and probably less effort and fear. Furthermore, trust that you will get there, even if you have the impression that you do not progress.

I: The most challenging phases for me were the practice sequences where I thought nothing was moving, and I wasn't making any progress. Of course, there are days when nothing seems to go right. But in a multitude of messages delivered to me by different mediums, the spirit world taught me that something was always unfolding, even if I didn't perceive it with my worldly senses.

I also had to get used to the idea that the other side also had to "practice" with me, i.e., my spirit friends needed my presence in various practice sessions to make progress with me on their side too. This idea comforted me and helped me not to give up, demotivated in moments I thought I did not progress.

I 24: When "Rudolph" first appeared, neither he, Martin, nor I were well aligned with one another. "Rudolph" needed time to adjust to working with Martin's body. In the early stages of our journey, he whispered more than he spoke clearly, and I could observe how he struggled to formulate even a single word. From my perspective, "Rudolph" spoke in an outdated version of German. His sentences were so long that I had difficulty following his philosophical dialogues. When I asked questions expecting pragmatic, down-to-earth answers with clear solutions, I often found myself disappointed.

Today, however, his speed of communication matches (and sometimes exceeds) the tempo of normal conversation. He uses modern words, and his sentences are typically much shorter. I have also come to understand that communicating with "Rudolph," as a representative of the "All-Oneness," doesn't mean he offers ready-made solutions in a fishbowl. Over time, I have become much more attuned to grasping the more profound meaning of his messages and sensing the underlying (healing) energies than I was at the beginning of our journey.

So, we ask you for a favor: take time in the coming weeks to set aside half an hour each day for these initial exercises, and, if possible, seek or create your own practice groups. From our side, we will guide and support you, and opportunities to practice will arise you are not yet aware of in this form. Of course, practicing in a group can help you to stay on the ball and not to withdraw with demotivation. For all those who are willing to embark on this medial journey not only alone, but together with others, the chapter "Shaping and Leading a Practice Group" may prove helpful.

1. Exercise:
Self-Awareness as the Foundation of Mediumship

In the first weeks of practice, we recommend sitting in silence, or as some call it, sitting "in one's own power." This does not mean you must be mentally silent. This is not possible at the beginning and, for many, may remain challenging throughout life. The goal here is to practice simply being yourself; thus, to listen inwardly, and to perceive how the physical and emotional body feels at this moment of time. You may also notice which thoughts are passing through your mind. There are many ways to consciously enjoy and experience this moment of silence. We will first describe a simple method that will help you to become more aware of all aspects of your body.

When you sit down (lying down at the beginning is less suitable because of the risk of falling asleep; standing works too, though it is less relaxing), we first ask that you sit comfortably and, if possible, upright. At the start of the exercise, pay attention to your motivation, as it will shape how the exercise unfolds. If you sit down intending to go deeper into meditation and learn something new about yourself, you will have a different experience than one motivated by obligation or discipline. From this moment on, you can trust that your intention will become reality.

Those who wish may ask us, the helpers from the other side, for support, so we may help you become calmer in your mind, more composed in dealing with your emotions, and more relaxed in your body. Because that is what we're here for: to make it as easy as possible for you to start communication with us from the spirit world. A false ambition of wanting to do everything alone so as not to be beholden to anyone is not helpful; after all, we are all connected to each other; your success is also ours.

In the first step, sit down and become aware of your body. It doesn't matter if you sense your entire body or just specific parts or regions. A single hand can be an interesting object of observation; exploring a hand with all its different sensations can be a rewarding and adventurous form of relaxation. It's beneficial to occasionally focus on different body parts since the more familiar you are with your body, the better you will be able to describe the physical sensations of the departed if they share their body perceptions with you.

For example, explore your right hand in your awareness: start with the wrist, feel to the right, to the left, identify how warm it is, and check if you sense a flowing or pulsing of the blood, and so on. Take your time with this. The more deeply anchored you are in your body, the more intensely we can work with you. Because you are then familiar with your physical sensations, you will be more alert to recognize any subtle changes in body experiences and strange, unfamiliar perceptions will not surprise you so easily anymore.

In the second step, we ask you to notice what you feel internally: Is there a little nervousness, a bit of tense curiosity? If so, you are like many others beginning this work; it is as though you are on a first date, unsure of what you are about to encounter. Similar emotional landscapes can arise when establishing a mediumistic contact with us.

Once you have recognized a feeling, perceive it in all its uniqueness, depth and beauty, just like the hand. Those who can, allow themselves to surrender and explore what it means to fully absorbed in this feeling. And for now, do not distinguish between so-called light-giving and darkness-creating emotions.

The first few weeks are about becoming familiar with the emotional states or "emotional players" within oneself, and to accept and appreciate these emotions in all their facets. Because greed, jealousy, hatred, and despair will also be emotions that are "transported" across you, for example, from the recipient to the spiritual being or vice versa. Especially because the deceased would like to have their own character portrayed (during their lifetime) and wants to use the medium's emotional clairvoyance to do so.

Those who resonate with these emotions themselves may distort the messages by intensifying, ignoring or even consciously suppressing them, as they do not feel comfortable experiencing these emotions themselves. Although it's important to experience and sense these emotions, it is equally essential not to resonate with them. This allows you to pass them on as desired emotions as purely, as possible or to dissolve them into neutrality for oneself, especially when they originate from the worldly recipient. Studying one's own emotionality and the emotionality of others is therefore a necessary preparation to later be able to cope with the emotional storms on both sides of the respective sender and receiver as a medium.

The third stage of this exercise is a little more challenging, as the focus is on your world of thoughts. We often work with your thoughts as inspiration. Therefore, it is more challenging for the medium to distinguish between thoughts that come from us and thoughts that arise from their own imaginative world thoughts. Alternatively, the medium may not be aware that he is reading the energy field of the recipient and has difficulties detecting that those thoughts are not coming from us, from the spirit world. The love for your own world of thoughts is what finally makes up your personality. And this is where you need to step back and get to know and appreciate this world of thought in all its diversity:

1. Which thought patterns are most familiar to me because I use them often?

2. Which language do I use?

3. How do I react internally to sudden external events?

These are aspects that need to be explored. This happens naturally when you, as a mediumistic traveler, allow yourself permission and space to explore these various states of being. Let your innate intuition guide you through each of these steps. It will provide you with the desired duration of the observation, but also the clarity of the respective aspects to be noticed.

Summary Exercise 1: Self-Awareness

a) Sit down quietly and remain in silence.
b) Start by observing one part of your body and explore it.
c) Focus on one of your emerging emotions. Immerse yourself in this one emotion and experience it in all its complexity and diversity.
d) Continue by observing your active mind. Look at your thoughts and notice your reactions. You don't need to judge them (though this may happen); simply acknowledge your current thoughts.
e) Finally, end the exercise by simply sitting still again and doing nothing.

2. Exercise:
Unfolding Your Heart to the Power of Love

We continually emphasize love as the foundation of mediumship work. Strengthening your own capacity for love is the focus of this next exercise. Here, you concentrate on unfolding your own love even further:

Sit quietly and let your thoughts drift. Observe your breath: breathe in and out calmly without trying to control it. Simply observe what happens, especially noticing without judgment how quickly your attention may wander, that is, how quickly you lose focus on your breath. This is a completely natural reaction at first; after all, you are used to seeking for new things in your everyday life, letting your gaze and therefore your attention wander. There is no need to be critical of yourself in this process.

As you observe your breath, be aware that there is nothing in this world that is not surrounded by the air you breathe in. Everything is enveloped by air. Everything that is alive breathes air in and out. Now imagine that everything you know is surrounded and permeated by air. Simply paint this scene in your mind.

With your next inhale, associate it with the idea that you are breathing in caring love. It is the divine care that enables you, through complex body processes, to breathe air. There is no place up to millions of light years away where you are so wonderfully nourished with caring air as here on earth. And this air is a form of love, a very caring love, full of abundance and diversity. Breathe it in with this awareness and simply breathe it out in silence. Breathe in the caring love and breathe it out again in silence. Recharge yourself with the caring love of the air—just let it happen—and breathe out silently.

As you breathe in, say inwardly, "I am breathing in the caring love of God/the power of creation" and "I am breathing out love". Whether you breathe in and out through your mouth or nose is secondary. The important thing here is to keep your focus on the fact that you are breathing in caring love.

Repeat this exercise as often as you can. This is an exercise you can do anywhere and anytime; you can do it while waiting at the bus stop, or in the morning when you wake up and feel like staying in bed a little longer.

The only challenge is to imagine that you are breathing in caring love and breathing love out in silence. Feel what is happening: whether you experience a different state of emotional awareness or even physical or visual experiences. Whatever happens, and even if nothing happens, simply stay focused by imagining breathing in and out caring love.

Summary Exercise 2: Unfolding Your Heart to the Power of Love

a) Sit quietly and observe how you breathe in and out.
b) Keep returning your attention to the inhalation and exhalation.
c) As you breathe, be aware that the same air you breathe in and out envelops and permeates everything in this world with its love.
d) Consciously breathe in this caring love.
e) Breathe out the caring love in silence.
f) Finally, end the exercise by simply sitting still again and doing nothing.

This exercise will help you understand that you have always been cared for, even if this has not always been the case in your everyday life. But it is true, and you can trust that you will continue to be cared for in the future. All experiences and learning tasks will be given to you while ensuring nothing can harm you, for you are lovingly cared for by what we call the power of creation or God.

3. Exercise:
Discovering Your Personal Spirit Guide

The question of connecting with your personal spirit guide also leads individuals to focus initially on exercises in which they learn to establish a direct connection with the spirit world. This is precisely the intention behind the following 3rd exercise. However, we ask all those seriously committed to the path of mediumship to do the Exercises he 1st and 2nd exercises regularly in the first few years. These will strengthen your body awareness and, in turn, your ability to develop love for yourself and everything that exists. Now, here's the classic exercise many mediums around the world practice again and again to strengthen contact with their spirit- guides and helpers:

Sit calmly and feel your body on all levels (see Exercise 1). Tune in and notice what your state of being is and who you are in this very moment. You will discover that this state varies and that there are only a few constants in your perception of your own personality. Take your time with this step and enjoy simply being in the moment.

Now, we ask you to imagine that you have an additional body around you, an energy body. Some call it the "aura field," but there is more to discover: simply imagine that you radiate energy from all parts of your body in all directions, as if you are forming a glowing, positively radiating egg around you. Feel this egg; let it expand and contract again. Do this exercise multiple times a day, preferably spread throughout the day so that you learn to feel comfortable in your own energy, your own power.

This "energy egg" serves as your mirror. When we speak of mirroring from now on, we mean that this mirror, or your energy field, can receive, or be "mirrored with," information originating from the spirit world. So, it may well be that later, during contact, you perceive something like a person before your mind's eye. Alternatively, emotions or voices might be projected into this mirror, which you then perceive on the corresponding channels. This egg-shaped mirror serves as a receiving station for everything that comes from the spirit world.

Like a normal mirror, this mirror can be more or less clear. The more you progress on your mediumistic journey, the clearer this mirror becomes. Initially, however, it resembles a pond surface that may only faintly reflect the events and character traits that we project into it. Once again, we encourage you to practice perceiving and expanding your energy mirror as often as you can.

Now, pause for a moment and direct your thoughts towards the spirit world. Imagine that you are taking on the role of a mediumistic phone. "Dial the number", that is, ask your spirit guide to step forward. May he reveal himself in your mirror and give you the opportunity to get to know him better. Wait and see what happens and focus your awareness on your different body levels (emotional, physical, mental and energy field).

If you do not perceive anything, that is good because then work is already being done on the spiritual side, and you will recognize an effect in later sessions. So, if you don't notice anything, sit in silence and notice yourself.

If you do perceive something, that is also good (not necessarily better). In this case, we ask you to notice everything what has changed within your body, what is different now. Please be fully aware of your own state and simply let whatever happens happen. Whenever you feel the urge to end this exercise, wait a little longer and then end it.

I: Staying a little longer may allow you to recognize your own inner resistances. It also gives your spirit guide the opportunity to work with you a bit more intensely.

You end the exercise by asking your spirit guide to step back and thanking them for supporting you and providing you the chance to get to know them. Imagine that this caring spirit guide was with you as a guest. Now accompany them to an imaginary exit with the same appreciation as you would with a dear friend. Because what you cherish will retain its value.

When the connection is over, observe your inner state and reconnect with your own body:

- How do I feel now?

- What am I sensing on the emotional level?

- How did I experience this exercise?

Then take a deep breath, focus on your feet, and feel the contact with the earth. Move your fingers and toes, stretch and reach out, and then slowly open your eyes and ease back into everyday consciousness at your own pace.

Summary Exercise 3: Discovering Your Personal Spirit Guide

a) Come into your own stillness (see Exercise 1)
b) Be aware of your body on all levels.
c) Visualize an energetic, radiant egg-shaped mirror around yourself.
d) Invite your designated spirit guide and get to know him/her by perceiving what is happening on all body levels.
e) End the contact by thanking them and saying goodbye to "your spirit guide."
f) Repeat steps d) and e) several times, paying attention to everything that happens or doesn't happen.
g) Tune into your body on all levels once more.
h) Gradually return to everyday consciousness at your own pace.

I: Gordon Smith encouraged us at the beginning of our training to write down everything we experience with the spirit world. We should pay particular attention to repetitions, such as where perception first changes and which patterns recur (warmth, cold, breeze, touch, etc.). He recommended keeping a journal for at least six weeks.

However, my experience has shown that it makes sense to write down your perceptions over a period of years, as the individual pieces often only come together into a meaningful whole after a long period of time. Over time, you get to know the preferred approach that your spirit helper consistently uses in order to connect to you. Gordon Smith calls this the "calling card" of your spiritual guide. Knowing the calling card of your spirit guide well helps you as mediums to feel assured that you are connected to the spirit world, even when you do not feel comfortable in your own skin or doubt your abilities.

My spirit helper, who works closely with me in a healing trance state, initially showed herself to me as follows: She made me feel as if both my hands and forearms were in a muff. These areas felt pleasantly warm on the outside, even though I usually have cold hands. Over the course of the exercise, I also had the impression that my hands and arms were not my own but belonged to another person.

Two years later, I received a confirming message from my teacher, Minister Matthew Smith —who was unaware of my prior sensations— that a nun was working closely with me as a spiritual helper. The "muff feeling" calling card suddenly made even more sense, as certain nun robes from earlier centuries included muffs that allowed them to keep their hands warm during winter prayers.

4. Exercise:
Strengthening your Mediumship through Self-Healing

While some of you have a spirit guide who stands by your side both as a mediumistic companion and in the role of a healer, there are others who perceive different types of personalities when receiving healing or working as a medium in other disciplines. The following exercise will help you to consciously notice this difference if it exists.

The next exercise turns out to be "tricky" if you don't carry it out exactly. We therefore ask you to carry out this exercise as it is presented:

Sit quietly and relax. Let your breath flow naturally. Observe how your breath flows in and out and relax your body from head to toe. Take your time with the relaxation; don't rush.

Now, ask the spirit world to connect you with your healer. This healing spirit has been nurturing, healing, and harmonizing you on your path for a long time. Don't question how this contact will happen. Instead, after setting your intention, allow that nothing seems to happen initially. Thus, focus then again on your breath and just wait.

You don't need to repeat your intention —just wait. There will come a moment (perhaps only after several attempts) when you notice a change in your body (warmth or cold) or in your emotionality (often inner tension, nervousness, or even fear), or, if you have experience here, also in your external energy field. Whatever happens, don't start judging it. Everything is just as it should be. Even if your pulse is beating up to your neck, and you break out in sweat, just allow it to happen. The spirit world is working more intensely with your body for the first time, so there may be responses in your personality that feel too strong or too mild initially. Be like a researcher and simply observe. That alone is difficult and may be a challenge for you.

For some of you, it is good to stop here after a while; you will notice that you simply no longer feel well. Then ask your spiritual, healing helper to step back or simply uninvite him or her (you are allowed to do this here), and thank them for practicing together and for the first steps you have taken together.

All those who do not feel too much discomfort in their physical, emotional, mental and energetic bodies despite a variety of unusual, i.e. uncontrollable reactions, can now take the next step:

Ask your spiritual healing guide —who knows you very well, has often served as a guardian angel, and has been there for you in a caring way— to give you healing. At first, please do not ask for anything specific; just ask for healing in general terms, and then wait again to see what happens. If nothing happens in your perception, then this is good. It is just as good if you perceive something on one of your body levels. Be certain, however, that healing is always sent; this happens regardless of whether your receiving antennae perceive it or not.

The love that is given to you with this healing strengthens you in your current state. It harmonizes you and will bring peace wher-ever you need it. Trust that something will change in the days following the healing and remain open to discover this change.

Here too, it is love that flows through everything, in this case the love of your spiritual healer, who has always been active for you and knows exactly what is good for you. Now you can perceive this healing love more precisely and more consciously and use it later, not only for yourself but also for others.

Enjoy this state for as long as you like, and when you realize that it is time to end this healing encounter, do so by thanking your healer and asking them to disconnect again. Then wait and observe whether and, if so, what changes in your perception on a physical, emotional, mental, and/or energetic level.

Then concentrate on your breath again before slowly awakening from your relaxation. Love guides and strengthens you; enjoy the change in perception as you open your eyes and stretch.

This exercise should be done almost daily at the beginning. Many of us who walk the earth have the impression that they have everything under control, that they are healthy and that they lack nothing. Only inner turmoil, outer dramas and physical illness lead to them being shaken out of this ignorant view. To demand healing for themselves and to regularly allowing yourself to heal is
another basic prerequisite for being able to practice your vocation as a medium in the long term in good health, with a happy heart and a clear, critical mind.

Let your love for yourself grow, for the brighter your inner fire, the greater your possibilities to ignite countless flames around you. Just as the light of a flame isn't dimmed by sharing, your light will not diminish when you begin to nourish yourself with love. It will enable you to share your light and love later with others.

Summary Exercise 4: Strengthening your Mediumship

a) Enter your own stillness (see Exercise 1).
b) Become aware of your body on all levels.
c) Imagine an energetic aura radiating from you in all direction and in the shape of an oval multidimensional mirror (Imagine yourself seated within the center of an egg-shaped cocoon of light.)
d) Invite your spirit healer and get to know him/her by comparing your previous, ordinary perception with what you perceive now.
e) First round: end the connection by thanking and respectfully bidding your spirit healer farewell.

f) <u>For advanced practitioners:</u> Ask your spirit healer to give you the healing he or she feels you need at this moment of time.

g) Observe if and what happens.

h) End the healing session by either asking your spirit healer to step back or realizing when the healing is over.

i) Tune in again to observe any changes on all levels of parts of your body, physically as well as emotionally.

j) Slowly, at your own pace, return to everyday consciousness.

5. Exercise:
Illuminating Your Mind

I: I first received this exercise in a light trance state, and I wrote the text on my laptop with my eyes closed. Yet, when I opened my eyes after 20 minutes of diligent typing, the Word document was still blank. As I tried this exercise several times for myself and found it very effective against my bad mood, I would like to share it with you here based on my memories:

Sit down, close your eyes, and relax. Breathe in and out deeply. Feel your feet on the ground and connect with the earth. Now turn your attention upward and imagine a beam of light, like a laser, is shining from above onto your third eye (an imaginary point slightly above between your eyebrows). Let it shine for a while, as if you were catching a ray of sunshine on a warm summer's day.

Imagine how this ray of light spreads across your scalp and makes your face, the top of your skull and the back of your head glow in its outermost layer of skin. Notice what happens, and let it flow naturally. Then imagine your entire brain filled with light, radiating.

45

In the next step, imagine all neural centers in your brain to glow from within. If you like, you can even imagine every gland in your head beginning to shine. Then simply passively perceive your illuminated head and wait to see what happens; you don't need to do anything else.

When you're ready to finish the exercise, take a deep breath in and out and draw your attention back on your feet. Move and stretch, and return to your normal, everyday awareness.

Summary Exercise 5: Illuminating Your Mind:

a) Enter your own stillness (see Exercise 1).
b) Feel your feet grounded on the earth.
c) Imagine a beam of light, like a laser, shining on your third eye.
d) Pause briefly before moving on.
e) Imagine this light beam spreading across your scalp... ...then let each of the individual convolutions of your cerebral corridors shine in full light.
f) Now all neural centers and glands start to light up from the inside.
g) Passively observe your illuminated head and wait to see what happens. You don't need to do anything else.
h) End the exercise by breathing deeply in and out, then focusing on your feet for a moment.

This exercise is especially helpful when you're feeling low or troubled by negative thoughts. For you as a medium, it's crucial to consistently raise your vibrational frequency, essentially improving your state of mind. On one hand, this elevates your energy, and on the other, it allows your spirit guides to connect with you more easily, enabling them to convey their messages with greater clarity.

6. Exercise:
Experiencing the Magnitude of Your Own Soul

Everything a medium is supposed to learn, it learns through messages and the feeling of what is being transmitted by us. Little, if anything, is learned with the help of the intellect only. The intellect is an organizing, structuring, and often controlling organ not well suited to fully grasp the magnitude of what takes place in
mediumistic work. Therefore, in the following exercise, we will engage in an experience that can help you make this transcendent magnitude more tangible:

Sit down and breathe in and out silently. Feel your whole body.

"Awaken" by noticing each part of your body parts one by one; the order is not relevant as much as thoroughness. Appreciate that everything works so well in your body, and give thanks for it, even if one or two things may not function as you would like them to. Because there are also forces at work here that at least ensure that you can continue to live in your physical form.

Do this for at least five minutes, i.e. longer than you would typically dedicate to such exercises. Being aware of your body helps you perceive the "shell" of your spiritual being. Only when you know your physical boundaries can you begin to soften and possibly even dissolve them.

Now, take a deep breath and, as you exhale, connect with what we call your "higher self", your great soul, which has united with your body to gather experiences on earth and work in ways that are impossible in the pure soul state.

Feel and let your great soul work. Try not to direct your attention with your intellect. If this happens, just take a few deep breaths in and out. And then, with a deep breath, continue to invite your great soul to make itself perceivable in you —in this, your body. Wait and notice what happens.

Enjoy this state and new sensations, take your time here. If thoughts appear and distract you, do not push them away, but simply return to observing your breath. Let whatever happens unfold naturally: If emotions arise, let them arise; if physical sensations like pain felt even more, notice that too. Should you have beautiful, unique experiences, allow them to flow without holding on to them. Simply exist in the greater self of your soul, in your divine being because that is what it is all about for the moment. Love will make itself known in various ways. So, explore what universal love is; it is at the core of your soul, continually working through you. Just be yourself, in your beingness, here on earth.

After a while, you will notice that your focus is waning. Then, bring your attention back to your breath and your body. Now observe what has changed in your body and allow everything to happen, including any sensations that arise once again. Do not rush out of the exercise but wait until it ends by itself.

Experiencing your divine being is more important than developing yourself and your mediumship with the help of your spiritual helpers. Anyone who succeeds in experiencing their own great power and the love of their own soul has the steadfastness to acquire for themselves the practice steps that are necessary to communicate with the spiritual world at a partnership level.

Because that is the main point here: we would rather not be perceived as higher powers or even worshiped. Yes, we also want to be treated with respect, but we are not on a higher level than you. We are not better, but we are not worse either. It is often very difficult for you on earth to admit to yourselves that you are all equal in a certain sense. No one is better, more right, or more beautiful. Partial aspects of you may be so in comparison, but what we call the human or soul being is not worth more or less than another.

Summary Exercise 6:
Experiencing the Magnitude of Your Own Soul:

a) Sit down and breathe in and out silently. Feel your whole body.
b) "Awaken" by becoming aware of each part of your body individually.
c) Appreciate that everything in your body works so well and give thanks for it.
d) Do this for at least five minutes.
e) Take a deep breath and, as you exhale, connect with what we call your "higher self" or your "great soul."
f) Wait a moment before you continue; feel your great soul and let it work.
g) Don't let your mind take over your attention. When this happens, consciously take a few deep breaths in and out.
h) Then, with a deep breath, continue to invite your great soul to make itself felt in you, your body.
i) When your focus is waning, bring your attention back to your breath and your body.
j) Observe what has changed in your body and allow everything to happen, including any sensations that arise once again.
k) Do not rush out of the exercise but wait until it ends by itself.

Your intellect won't be able to fully understand this path of mediumship with all its insights, and sometimes even consciously not understand it. After all, the usual thought patterns are such that they are reduced to absurdity with the new inner attitude and mindset shaped by the medium. But only equality between partners enables complete trust. This is especially important in mediumistic communication with departed or other spiritual beings. Love flows purely only when there is no "higher" and no "lower", no "better" or "worse." And one's own healing can only succeed completely if the spiritual healer and the recipient of healing do not think and act in judgmental categories.

Only the experience of your own great power and love, your own immeasurable magnitude, can fundamentally break down the mental concept. So, do practice this exercise as often as you can, and you will become a pure channel through which love, and mediumistic messages can flow particularly easily.

7. Exercise:
Emotional Growth as a Gateway to Mediumship

Now we will focus on the ability to receive different types of information. The range of information that can be transmitted will be expanded.

Now that you have been doing the previous exercises for a long time, your body will relax naturally during the exercises. Little effort is needed; you're already used to relaxing. On days when your mind is overly active due to outside events, start with Exercise 1 before beginning this one.

To begin with, sit quietly and relaxed and feel your body. From this deep relaxation, ask for your spirit guide —the being who has been working closely with you recently. Feel its presence, feel its form of existence within you, and allow your perceptions to completely envelop you.

You are now ready to communicate more closely with your spirit guide. Ask it to lead you to a life event which happened in your past. After you have set this intention, let go and wait to see what happens. Whatever comes up, don't judge the event. Don't think:

"No, I don't want that, I want something different, something better," or "Not this again; I have had enough of it." Trust that your spirit guide will choose what is most relevant for your continued spiritual development at this moment.

Then let yourself be guided into the event. You may see images or scenes; you may hear yourself or others speak or experience the same thoughts you had back then. You might even feel the physical sensations of that past moment. Whatever it is, let it unfold. If emotions arise, let them come, and if you find they are too intense, ask your spirit guide to take them from you. They will gratefully take them and bring you relief. If helpful, you can imagine your guide absorbing these emotions, images, or perceptions and dissolving them in the light.

The important thing here is that you learn to allow that there are events in your life that can be looked at again, for whatever reason. And that, if you wish, spirit guides stand by to take from you anything that feels too much, too negative, or too difficult for you. Because as a child of God, which we all are, you can carry heavy things, but you don't have to. It is therefore important that you learn to experience this relief for yourself.

Note that this exercise is not only for negative or emotionally charged situations. Positive, joyful, and happy moments may also arise. Examine these moments closely and observe your reactions. People often find it easier to accept difficult or challenging moments, yet happy and cheerful ones are often harder to endure when you do not see yourself as a being of light and instead identify with the heaviness. This does not mean that we wish to turn you into arrogant beings, but only that we want to show you how great you already are in this life, in your being, and how much love, joy and happiness you can experience if you allow yourself to indulge in positive memories once again.

Your love for yourself determines your spiritual growth, while fear of whom you once were holds you back from fully living your potential with joy and ease However, this is what this exercise is about; this is what we want to achieve with you because love makes you grow. Fear, like clouds, makes love invisible to you, but fear cannot erase or suppress love.

I: As a medium, we are not only confronted with our own emotionality, but very often also with the emotions of the sitter. When I realize that this emotionality is getting too much for me, I ask my spirit guides for help. They are then happy to become active so that the emotional situation begins to clear up.

A long time ago, I had a discussion with a good friend about this. She believed we should only call our spirit guides in an emergency and first use all our abilities to resolve a situation ourselves. She believed that if we asked others for help, we would be responsible for abdicating our own duty. I only share this view to a limited extent. Of course, everyone can first try to solve the situation on their own using their own skills. However, my spirit guides and various teachers point out that spirit guides are pleased to support us. Some believe that our own spirit guides can also grow with us in their spiritual development if we give them the chance to support us.

Another perspective I nurture is, that false pride or fear should not prevent us from asking for help when it is needed. Especially when I convey mediumistic messages, it's not primarily about having to endure and immediately transform the initial emotional state of my recipients. Instead, the focus should be on being as clear a channel as possible or acting as a well-functioning mediumistic "telephone". In my view, there is no imbalance in the sense of our partnership if I also ask for the help of my spirit guides in everyday life. On the contrary, everyone involved ultimately makes themselves available for the service of conveying divine love and the eternity of life.

Summary Exercise 7: Emotional Growth

a) Sit down and relax.
b) Invite your spirit guide.
c) Set your intention: Show me a situation from my past life.
d) Immerse yourself in this situation and perceive it on all levels of your body.
e) If an experience is too emotionally heavy to bear, pass it on directly to your spirit guide.
f) Practice this exercise regularly, as growing self-love in personal life leads to greater clarity and emotional balance during your mediumistic work.

8. Exercise:
Recognizing Different Spirit Guides

We are now beginning an exercise to help you learn more about your spirit guides. We refer to them in the plural, even though many of you may work with only one spirit guide. This spiritual being may have lived on earth multiple times, which means your guides may present themselves in different qualities. Once you have established your own light-filled energies (Exercise 5), it is helpful to focus on sensing the presence of the spirit guide currently working with you.

To accomplish this, we ask you to sit down and relax. Then, expand your corona into a full body "energy screen", making it as wide and expansive as you comfortably can. This requires only your intention, not so much an actual active will. Any ambition is improper; playful ease is the quality with which we can work particularly well.

Now, invite your spirit guide—the spiritual being who has been working closely with you for a long time and who has brought you to this moment in your life. Sense his/her presence with calm and patience. Now ask this helper to show you something that you have not yet learned about him. This could be a description of their
previous outward appearance, new character traits or experiences from their earthly life. He or she may also show you on a map where he or she has lived or give you street names, family names or similar. Whatever it is, remain open to it. After the exercise, make a note of what you have learned about your faithful spiritual helper.

In a next step, ask your spirit guide to step aside. Request that another spiritual being, one you have not worked with before, introduce themselves. Simply observe what happens.

- How does your body perception change?

- What happens to your emotions, do they stay the same or do they change?

- How do thoughts, or images, arise?

- Which names appear, and how do they relate to what you learn about this new entity?

- Is there a connection between you and this new being?

- Is it possibly a distant relative?

- Is it a spiritual being who always appears for specific purposes or tasks (e.g., organization, healing, communication, relaxation)?

- What task does this being had in your life?

- What gifts might she/he impart to you?

Whatever you are experiencing now and whatever new thing you are experiencing, simply perceive it and take it in. Then, ask this spiritual entity to step aside and spend a moment in your own presence before inviting your faithful spirit guide back. Now also perceive this spirit guide once more in all clarity. Note how this spirit helper differs from the previous being. What distinguishes your spiritual helper in particular?

This contrast or comparison helps you identify new aspects for recognizing your spirit guides. The aim isn't to get to know the second guide extensively, but to deepen your understanding of the guide who works closely with you. This recognition gives you confidence in times of uncertainty. Practicing will also help you to become familiar with how it feels when both spiritual helpers are present. This may well be the case later, when you are working as a medium and several spiritual beings want to communicate with you at the same time.

If you like, you can switch back to the second guide and repeat the exercise as described. Alternatively, you can also return to your normal everyday consciousness. Remember to thank and respect-fully release each spirit guide before ending your connection.

I: During our several years of training, we encountered differing views on the nature and number of spirit guides with whom a medium works. Gordon Smith places great importance on thoroughly getting to know your "main spirit guide," how he calls your primary spirit helper, before working intensively as a medium. He believes that generally, one spirit guide works closely with a medium from the beginning to the end of the mediumistic path.

Other mediums propose that some people may not have any spirit guide at all at their side. This is particularly the case if the person is far from being able to react to the influence of their spiritual helpers. The question here is: Why would spirit guides engage with someone who is not receptive or aware of their efforts?

Some teachers assume that you can have a whole team at your side during your mediumistic journey. This team supports you depending on the task and discipline; there are helpers who are always part of the core team; others only work with you for certain times and then leave this core team. From the very beginning, Martin worked reliably with one spirit guide, and he got to know him more and more thoroughly and comprehensively over the year.

M: I first consciously encountered my spirit guide (looking back, I can recognize this now) during a week —long seminar called "Unfolding Love: The Quadrinity Process" by Bob Hoffmann. Some condemn this process while others praise it, but for me, it brought beautiful experiences. During a "chocolate meditation," I sensed a radiant being behind me, far larger than myself, with enormous wings. Initially, I thought it was Archangel Michael, but upon seeing an additional set of wings, I realized it was a cherub. This vision was powerful, supportive, and filled me with courage. However, over time, the memory faded, and I rarely felt that connection again.

Then, years later, I was guided to my spirit helper via the trance state by Sandie Baker during a week —long seminar at the Arthur Findlay Colleague. I recognized the strong light energy that strengthened my back and remembered my first contact, which was a long time ago. But this time my spirit helper appeared as a major, a war hero. I could perceive him clearly and see him in my mind's eye, and I was uncomfortable being connected to the military. However, he wanted to show himself to me, and in one of the next sessions he provided further "proof". At the "automatic writing" exercise with a planchet (= mediumistic writing instrument), he guided my hand, and I wrote down the following note: "I am here, Major!" —but upside down and backwards! I did not read it the first time. I was only able to read the scribble when I held the note in front of a mirror; then it flashed through me. Okay, I had understood: "He" was there, and I could accept him from now on.

Years later, Matthew Smith once again reconnected me with my spirit guide through several sessions. I was able to describe in detail the region in which he lived, where he lived, the span of his life, and his appearance. I was particularly impressed by the windows and doors of his house. Matthew was able to confirm every detail.

Many people believe they work with multiple helpers, but I feel connected to just one spirit who shows up in different forms. The energy I sense each time remains consistent, with only the appearance changing. Matthew once told me that spirit guides show up in forms we can accept without fear. So, a first appearance might be as a dog, cat, or child, with the full form revealed only later. For me, the cherub appearance was essential to trust and open —up to my spirit guide and the spirit world.

I: The cooperation with my spirit guides first developed during an exercise in a seminar by Gordon Smith. First a male spirit guide came through, whom I was able to perceive well because of his weight and size even when I was not one hundred percent focused (which was the norm rather than the exception at the beginning). The initial evidence from Gordon Smith and Steven Levett confirmed the presence of a male spirit guide; however, their very different and rather confusing descriptions didn't really make sense until many years later...

Iris 24: ...During one of our practice exercises, this male spirit guide shared his first name with me: "Paul." Almost a decade later, I discovered that the spiritual entity "Rudolph" was also named Paul during his time on earth. It was his first name. In the early years, "Paul" often spoke through me when I entered a trance state. His messages were frequently profound, addressing meaningful and life-philosophical topics —just as they are today when "Rudolph" works through Martin. In addition, he is one of the spirit teachers who has taken great joy in helping us write our books and facilitating our regular mediumistic practice groups. In Germany.

You might ask: Is "Rudolph" a single spirit guide serving both of us? To be honest, we don't know for certain. However, in one of Martin's early trance sessions, "Rudolph" explained that "All-Oneness" had lent the personality of "Rudolph" to communicate with us and share his wisdom with all who are interested.[1]

I: But "Paul" was not my only spiritual companion. Just a few months later, in mediumistic exercise groups, several people independently of each other confirmed that I had another spirit guide; they noticed a woman with a hairstyle that was piled up about 40 cm high. Anyone who knows me well, knows that I'm not a fan of complex hairstyles and that I don't enjoy working intensively with my hair. However, despite this aversion, I followed up on the clues and regularly sat down in silence to contact her. Not only did she consistently reach out to me with a specific "calling card" that I recognized, but I also noticed that she worked closely with me in active mediumistic communication and supported me with other, often work-related, everyday matters.

Summary Exercise 8: Recognizing Different Spirit Guides:

a) Sit down calmly and relax.
b) Expand your corona into a large, wide energy screen.
c) Invite your spirit guide and sense his full presence.
d) Now ask your spirit guide to step aside and invite another, still unknown spirit entity to introduce oneself.
e) Observe everything that happens. (Optionally, note your perceptions after the exercise.)
f) Then, ask this spirit helper to step aside as well, and take a moment to rest in your own presence.
g) Now invite your first spirit guide to return; perceive him clearly.

---

[1] Iris & Martin Magin (2020) „Nachrichten aus der Anderen Welt", Volumen 1-5

h) Pay close attention and explore how your spirit guide differs from the new spirit helper.
i) You can now switch back and forth between the two spiritual beings, in this way and explore the differences for as long as you like.
j) End the exercise by thanking both spirit guides and gradually return to your everyday consciousness.

I 24: As a skeptic by nature, I sought confirmation of my spirit guides from others, such as experienced mediums and mediumistic practice partners. Over time, I received descriptions and even names for my various spirit guides. Today, I believe I work with a core team of spirit guides. Depending on the mediumistic discipline or life task, I feel the presence of some of them more strongly as others. Nowadays, at the start of our 5th year of our weekly "Rudolph" dialogues through Martin, I must admit that I do know more about "Rudolph's" life experiences and philosophical views, than from any other spirit guide working with me closely.

9. Exercise:
Connecting with Departed Loved Ones

Now that you have expanded your energy field (aura field) and have learned to work together with different spirit guides from your helper team, the time has come to consciously experience receiving deceased individuals who were previously either not connected to you at all or were on the fringes of your acquaintances.

To accomplish this, sit down again and relax. Be aware that this exercise is also just an experiment; an exercise, nothing more. As long as you maintain this attitude, you will be filled with trust, light, and love; in this state, anything is possible.

Build up your own radiant energy field (aura). Imagine that it surrounds you like the form of an egg and radiates love and light through you. Now ask your spirit guides to send you a guest, i.e., someone who has recently passed away. Wait and see what happens. It helps if you envision this "spirit guest" entering through an imaginary door and connecting with you through your "energy egg" to communicate with you.

Notice how your own physical perception changes as your "spirit guest" connects with you:

- Does your body feel bigger or smaller?

- Do your shoulders widen or slump forward?

- How big is your abdominal circumference now?

- How long are your fingers?

- Can you perceive the shape of a face — the eyebrows, the size of the mouth, perhaps a beard or a particularly prominent nose, etc.?

- Do you feel more the energy of a woman or that of a man?

Perceive the connection to your "spirit guest'" and whatever you perceive, simply allow it. When you are ready, express aloud what you perceive. The next step is to learn more about this deceased person: You may find out what kind of person he or she was:

- What personality does your "spirit guest" possess?

- Was he or she more of a quiet observer or a very communicative and lively character?

- Was he or she more of a sober, matter of fact type or a quick tempered, emotional one?

Allow your spirit guest to share their story in the way they choose. You are also welcome to inquire about aspects of their life internally, such as:

a) Were you married, and did you have a family of your own?

b) What profession did you pursue?

c) What were your favorite leisure activities?

d) Where did you live? (Small room, larger apartment, own house, type of furniture, ...?)

e) What was your place of residence like? (Village, small town or bigger city?)

f) What technical items were available in your time? (Car, washing machine, telephone, television, computer, hairdryer, motorcycle, motorboat, ...?)

g) What clothes did you prefer to wear? (Did you value good and neat clothing at all?)

h) Which dishes did you particularly enjoy?

As you can see, there are countless aspects to explore here. At the end of your encounter, ask your spirit-guest what the reason for his/her appearance is. Often a message will emerge, or a symbol will be handed over that may have a meaning for you. Whatever it is, acknowledge it, and thank him/her for what he/she has given you.

When closing the exercise, thank the deceased for coming and consciously say goodbye to him/her. Enjoy your own body awareness for a moment before opening your eyes and gradually returning to your everyday consciousness.

If you like, you can place a recording device next to you during such encounters and record what is said. But for this first time, it is enough that you learn to invite various deceased people yourself and to feel their presence.

I: Many of our teachers (Eileen Davis, Steven Levett, Gordon Smith, Matthew Smith, Jill Parker and others) have pointed out to us how important mutual respect is when working with beings from the other world. This is not only about establishing respectful contact with our Spirit guides, but also about not suddenly breaking off contact at the end of a joint project. After all, abruptly breaking off contact when you are a guest at someone's home, or worse still, suddenly complimenting your own guests out, would also appear impolite in our world.

Summary Exercise 9: Connecting with Departed Loved Ones

a) Sit down and relax. Be aware that this exercise is only an experiment.

b) Expand your energy field into a large, enveloping, glowing energy egg.

c) Now ask your spirit guides to send you a guest who has recently passed away. You can imagine that this guest enters through an imaginary door.

d) Notice how your physical perception changes (size, girth, facial features, feet/hands, etc.).

e) Then allow yourself to learn about the personality and/or life of the deceased.

f) Take in everything that happens.

g) If you wish, say out loud what you perceive and pay attention to whether you hear the reason for this contact (message or symbol). Thank yourself for it.

h) The exercise is finished when the departed soul steps back. Thank your spiritual guides and slowly return to your everyday consciousness.

Of course, it is difficult at the beginning to determine whether your guest, the deceased, really experienced everything that you think you perceived. This requires a counterpart (e.g., a practice partner) who can provide clarifying answers to the evidence the spirit world has given to you as a medium. But this is not necessary at this stage. Learn to simply speak and concentrate on what comes through. Sense and explore the different states of your own being and that of the spiritual being working with you.

The following applies to all exercises: explore the different types of transmission that the spirit world uses to train you as mediums. Wish for the greatest possible openness and spirit of research; that is all that is necessary. Do not allow yourselves to be distracted by doubts after practicing, as this is not conductive to achieving your goals. You can be assured that your discipline in practicing your mediumship over a longer period will pay off.

With this in mind, we wish you many wonderful guests from the spirit world and much joy in getting to know each other.

10. Exercise:
Exploring Your Personal Mission

At a certain point, everyone reaches a place where they can ask themselves: Why do I want to be a medium? What truly drives me? This is the subject of the following exercise, which is short but of central importance for your spiritual development.

Sit down and take a deep breath in and out. Let your thoughts wander for a moment, then relax as you normally would.

Now, ask your spirit guides to lead you into an even deeper state of relaxation. Wait and observe what happens.

If you find it difficult to release your thoughts at this point in time, consider trying this exercise at another moment.

But once you have found a deeper level of relation than you are familiar with, ask yourself: What is truly important in my life? Wait for the answer that develops within you.

Then ask yourself: What mission do you, my spirit guides, want to fulfill together with me in this lifetime? Then wait and observe what you perceive and what insights you gather.

Now, continue to be inspired by asking for a gift, a present that the spirit world would like to give you; this gift could appear in the form of a symbol, for example. This symbol is an aid; it reminds you again and again in the coming time that you do not have a mission alone, but that others from the spirit world are also working with you to fulfill this mission.

When you're ready, thank your spiritual guides for the gift and gradually return to your everyday consciousness. Sit in silence for a while before you open your eyes and return to the everyday challenges of your life.

Summary Exercise 10: Exploring Your Personal Mission

a) Sit down, breathe in and out deeply, let your thoughts wander, and relax.
b) Ask your spirit guides for even deeper relaxation and wait to see what happens.
c) Once you reach a deeper level of relaxation, ask: What is truly important in my life?
d) Wait for your spirit guide's response.
e) Now ask: What mission would you, my spirit guides, want to fulfill together with me at this time?
f) Wait for the answer, notice everything, and gather insights.
g) Request a gift from the spirit world and wait for it to appear.

> h) Thank your spiritual guides and return to your every-
>   day consciousness.
> i) Sit in silence for a while before opening your eyes.
>   You can repeat this exercise from time to time.

If you feel uncertain or doubt the authenticity of what arises within you, ask the spirit world to give you signals in daily life. This could be a friend's comment, an event you witness on the street, or a sentence you read somewhere. Whatever it is, remember that nothing (from the spirit world) is being done to unsettle you. All is intended to give you greater confidence and assurance.

Record your insights once again and celebrate your progress in mediumistic work, as from now on, your growth will likely be more abundant than you have previously experienced.

11. Exercise:
Strengthening Your Spirit Communication

In this exercise, you will practice connecting with the spirit world once more, but this time differently:

Sit down and relax in your usual way. Breathe in and out, allowing your thoughts to drift away. Establish a presence in your body by becoming fully aware of each sensation.

Once you feel calm and centered, connect with your spirit guide. Spend a moment simply feeling his/her presence for a while before moving on.

Now, ask the spirit world to share with you a song, a philosophical text, a quote, a mantra, or something similar. Make a brief request and wait to see what happens.

Once you have received a sentence (*song*, etc.), notice what reactions the message triggers in you: Do you see images? Do emotions arise? Do inspiring thoughts appear? Whatever happens, observe it for a while.

Then ask your spirit guide to share the reason for this particular message: "Why did you choose to share this (sentence, image, emotions) with me?" Pause and allow any answers to come.

In the second step, ask: "What significance does this message have from your perspective, and what prompts you to give it to me today, at this precise moment?" Again, wait and see what emerges.

Whatever meaning, reason, or timing behind the message, simply acknowledge it and enjoy the communication with your Spirit guides; because that is what it is all about now.

If not yet answered, ask: "What healing message lies within this?"

Request that the spirit world reveal the full beauty of what they have conveyed to you. Enjoy and immerse yourself in all the beauty that is then shown to you, remaining connected to the phrase, quote, song, or message that was given to you.

In this way, you can continue communicating with your spiritual guides in your unique way, practicing playfully for a while.

Close the connection as usual and enjoy the presence in your own body for a while. Then open your eyes and write down the entire experience.

Summary Exercise 11: Strengthen Your Communication

k) Sit down and relax in the usual way.
l) Build presence in your body by perceiving everything clearly.
m) Connect with your spirit guide. Feel its presence for a while before you continue.
n) Now ask your spirit guide for a song, a philosophical text, a quote, or a mantra. Wait, to receive it.
o) Once you've received a message, observe the reactions it creates within you —any images, emotions, or thoughts.
p) Ask your spirit guide for the reason for this particular message and wait for a response.
q) Follow up with the question, "What is the meaning of this message (song, etc.) from your perspective, and why did you choose to deliver it to me at this time?"
r) Ask if there is an underlying healing message of what has been transmitted.
s) Request to see the full beauty of what has been transmitted.
t) Enjoy and immerse yourself in this experience.
u) Continue communicating playfully with your guides, practicing this connection.
v) Close the connection to your spirit guide as usual, by showing your gratitude.
w) Finish the moment by slowly returning to your everyday consciousness.
x) Sit in silence for a while before you open your eyes
y) Open your eyes and write down your experiences and insights.

12. Exercise:
Collecting your Mediumistic Benefits

In this exercise, you will explore the question of how mediumship has personally benefited you so far.

To do this, we ask you to sit down, find your inner calm, and relax. Let go of anything that burdens you in daily life; relax both your physical and emotional bodies; if possible, let go of any lingering thoughts.

Now, connect with your spirit guides and ask them to form a deep, intense connection with you. Let their love and presence envelop you; fully immerse yourself in this experience.

Then ask your spirit guides to show you what has changed in your life since you have been practicing regular discipline. Take a close look at the events they show you and notice what emotions they trigger in you and what insights you gain from them. The events may appear as single moments, details, or as a flow of life sequences, giving you an overview of all you've experienced on your mediumistic journey.

Take it all in and observe what this reflection on your spiritual journey so far does to you. Consider whether you've gained new experiences that have benefited you. See how your trust in what we call the 'spirit world' has grown, and see how this has changed your relationships in life by asking yourself:

- "How do I now respond to others? How do others respond to me?

- What attitude have I developed towards the work I do every day?

- To what extent has my attitude changed?"

Simply notice how you have progressed on this mediumistic journey. If you wish, feel free to write down any insights and realizations. But remember that the more important aspect is to do these exercises again and again until you arrive at a complete picture of your spiritual unfolding.

When practicing alone, it's challenging to gauge your own progress. If you don't take a break every now and then, you won't be able to assess your level of development well. Now is the time to take stock, to see whether the journey into which you have invested so much time truly aligns with your life, brings you joy, and whether you really wish to continue with this mediumistic discipline.

Thank your spiritual guides for all they have shown you and gradually return to your everyday consciousness.

If you like, look at your notes again and again over the coming days, recapitulate your experiences from the past weeks or months and gather insights from them.

Summary Exercise 12: Collecting your Mediumistic Benefits

a) Sit in silence and establish your energy field.
b) Connect with your spirit guide.
c) Ask for an especially deep connection. Let yourself be enveloped in their love and immerse yourself in this experience.
d) Then, ask your spiritual guide to show you how your life has changed since you began practicing regularly.
e) Take a closer look at the events shown, notice the emotions they evoke, and draw conclusions from yourself.
f) Reflect on any new experiences you have gathered on your mediumistic journey that have benefited you:

- How did your trust in your friends from the spirit world developed?
- How do you react to others today?
- How do others respond to you?
- What relationship have you built up with your daily work?
- What has changed?

g) Just notice how you have evolved on your mediumistic journey.
h) Bid farewell to your spiritual guides, thanking them for everything.
i) Gently return to your everyday consciousness.

Taking Time to Rest on Your Mediumistic Journey

Once you have completed these 12 practice exercises, you will have reached a point where you have established the foundations for communicating with the spirit world. It is as if you have finished your first year of school after all that dedicated practice. Now, you have the opportunity —indeed, a valuable chance— to view everything you have done and experienced from a broader perspective.

Now is the time to take a break from your mediumistic exercises! Treat yourself to at least a four-week break, but ideally, aim for six weeks of "mediumistic summer vacation" before you return to your mediumistic work. During this "mediumistic-free" time, pay close attention to whether you feel anything missing in your everyday life.

This break is important so that you can integrate everything you have learned so far into your personal life. It is not just about developing the gift of acting as a mediumistic telephone in formal practice situations. No, it is about learning how to use your mediumistic abilities in normal everyday life. However, this will happen naturally and often unconsciously. Now is the time to take a step back from your mediumship practice for a while, to let go and open yourself up to all the new challenges and experiences that life offers you.

I: Our mentor, Matthew Smith, emphasized the importance of taking breaks after extended practice sessions. From my standpoint, this helped me to keep checking my own motivation and to see whether I wanted to give higher priority to other issues in my current life. Moreover, I could test the insights I gained in the mediumistic practice spaces to see how applicable they were to my daily life, which further built my personal trust in the messages I received.

If you have been practicing the exercises we introduced with discipline and consistency, your trust has likely grown to the point where you now know —rather than merely believe— that your spirit guides are indeed walking with you, guiding and supporting you on your path. For each of you, this journey may look different: those who feel called to continue down the mediumistic path will receive the guidance and inspiration they need. For others, this mediumistic journey may have been just a meaningful chapter within their personal journey.

Thanks to the skills you have acquired, you can now connect with your spirit guides at any time. With the knowledge and experience that there are also spiritual beings who can help you or others in your environment.

Chapter IV:

Shaping and Leading a Spiritual Practice Group

In this chapter, we want to share our experiences in setting up mediumistic practice groups with you and give you tips in case you, like us, are faced with the task of leading such a group one day.

Who hasn't experienced this? After returning from a seminar, you're filled with intentions to practice regularly and integrate the new teachings into daily life. But then, when you're on your own again at home, it's often difficult to find the necessary discipline and motivation to practice regularly. For some, doubt even starts to creep in-questioning whether what they learned will actually work for them. During these moments of discouragement, it's easy to let the self-imposed learning discipline slip away.

Ramadahn, an inspiring entity from the spiritual realm, has conveyed through the renowned English medium Ursula Roberts the importance of joining a group to further one's growth, both as a person and as a spiritual being (Ramadahn Trust (2006), Volume 6, pp. 37–39): A group can help keep you going, even when the initial enthusiasm or drive for growth in your chosen discipline wanes. The group is the "place" where the weak help the strong to develop their understanding and the weak give the strong the opportunity to serve, according to Ramadahn. The strong, in turn, help the weak through their encouragement, knowledge, and insights.

Ramadahn also emphasizes that part of inner growth occurs in solitude and silence, such as during meditation or prayer. But the real character strengthening happens when you are with others, when you are part of a group or a family.

When you're alone, no one witnesses the efforts you put in, which can sometimes make you feel inadequate or weak. How different it is when like-minded people notice your efforts, honor the small and large successes in your development, and reflect them back. Ramadahn points out how important this mutual encouragement is to persevere, to be able to deal patiently and understandingly with one's own stumbles, falls, and weaknesses.

A spiritual practice group provides this support and offers a space to encourage each other, develop understanding, and be there for one another in a spirit of service. It also creates an opportunity to explore different areas of spiritual practice in a playful, experimental way and experience oneself in them. It is precisely in the interaction and confrontation with different personalities and their emotionality and expectations, your own spiritual skills and character are truly tested.

After a break of about four to six weeks, you might feel a yearning to continue exploring this path with your spiritual guides. At that point, it may be the right time to step beyond individual practice and seek practice partners and sometimes, they simply appear in your life. If you are wondering where the opportunities to practice should come from, simply trust the spiritual guidance, which will provide you with the appropriate support.

However, be prepared to make a personal commitment. Often, this initially involves traveling longer distances to connect with other mediumistic practice groups. But it also means a considerable effort if you then decide to set up a regional practice group yourself.

Facilitating Growth as a Group Leader

During our training with Gordon Smith, we were asked by other participants quite early on to shape and lead a mediumistic practice group. Under the misconception we needed to be highly experienced professional mediums first, it took us a few months before we took the plunge. Thankfully, other participants and Gordon himself encouraged us so kindly that we couldn't refuse but take on the role of a practice group leader together.

From the start, we wanted to work in a partnership-based way, meaning that all group members are equals on the mediumistic development path, and that we, as group leaders, are not teachers but see ourselves in the role of facilitators. We emphasize this point regularly. Each participant is fully responsible for their own spiritual development and mediumistic practice experience. This also means that we as group leaders accept no liability for any aftereffects or even negative health or psychological consequences.

When questions arise, we answer them based on our own current experience and knowledge level. We make it clear from the outset that there are many different perspectives and that we ourselves are not professional mediums. In the early years, we only provided corrective feedback when our group's guiding principles (to give you an idea, please see next page) were violated or when someone was behaving destructively. Today, 12 years of leading mediumistic practice groups later, we do sometimes fall in the mode of teaching occasionally, each of us two sharing our unique mediumistic insights.

Especially when forming a new mediumistic practice group, we recommend that you reflect on the principles you want your group's cooperation to be based on if you decide to (co-)found or lead a group by yourself or together with a co-facilitator. Our experience is that the introduction of such basic mediumistic principles creates an additional seriousness regarding practicing together. Furthermore, new participants can be quickly informed by providing these principles (digitally or on paper), so that they can onboard and integrate more quickly. This eliminates the need for lengthy explanations and therefore time-consuming explanations of the set-up at the beginning of each practice session.

Foundational Principles for Mediumistic Collaboration:

- We meet to unfold together with our spiritual friends.
- Our meetings are experimental in nature, meaning no specific outcomes (e.g., healings) can be expected.
- We remain aware that we're in a learning environment, allowing ourselves, as practitioners, to make mistakes and gain experiences.
- Each of us is responsible for ourselves and our own development.
- This means that in situations that disrupt our well —being, the disruptive factors are addressed or tackled to improve them if necessary.
- Since we are all student, teachers, and learners simultaneously (including Martin and Iris), we encourage everyone to provide feedback to one another.
- Please be punctual. We close the doors five minutes after the start to create a closed and highly vibrating practice room.
- We recommend that everyone cultivates positive and constructive thoughts before and upon entering the room.
- Messages that come from the spirit world are always of a positive, supportive and uplifting nature. They are accompanied by an energy of a caring, peaceful or loving nature and can be recognized precisely by this.
- We are aware of how quickly our imagination can mislead us so that our messages do not come from a spiritual source but rather from our own personality or ego. Therefore, listeners have the responsibility to carefully gather evidence that the messages actually come from another (spiritual) level. Providing this feedback of these affirming messages creates trust for both the sender and the receiver.
- We understand that medical diagnoses, negative messages, and obligatory instructions are not content from the spirit world. If these appear, all participants should regard them as misinterpretations and disregard them. Anyone who doesn't respect this rule will be excluded from our practice group.
- If you receive a prophecy or other future-oriented messages, remember that we are all students, and these messages may not always be accurate.
- Make sure you drink plenty of water, especially after deeper trance sessions.
- If you feel unwell after a session, feel free to stay and rest before heading home.
- Intense sessions may have aftereffects. Take the time you need at home to recharge and find a retreat if necessary.

Crafting Your Practice Group's Purpose and Structure

What we underestimated at the start was the positive and profound impact of having a clear intention for the purpose of the group. This intention influences the choice of exercises and the framework in which they are held.

Before we focus on the mediumistic exercise group in the following, a brief digression: In addition to groups that are physically present, it is also possible to conduct exercise groups via telephone or video conferences. While aspects such as premises and catering are then eliminated, these forms of training do influence the selection of exercises and the manner of our group facilitation.

For our practice groups, we distinguish between the following types in general:

Experimental Practice Groups: These groups provide a space to explore various exercises. The goal of these groups is to open up new horizons of experience in a playful and easy way.

Developmental Practice Groups: Participants meet with the specific goal of growing spiritually together over a longer period. These groups are more focused; members come together at a set time (often weekly) to work on a specific mediumistic theme or area of growth.

Common themes that a dedicated practice group might focus on include:

- *Spiritual healing*
- *Inspirational (mediumistic) speaking and writing*
- *Spiritual assessment*
- *Classical mediumship (communication with the deceased)*
- *Trance/Entrancement*
- *Physical mediumship*

The type of practice group that's right for you depends not only on your personal preferences but also on the interests of the group members. An experimental exercise group is recommended as a starting point. If several participants are willing and able to muster the discipline, the transition to a development exercise group can take place.

We ourselves set up a fixed group of participants (development exercise group) and were able to see the positive effect after a few weeks: This created a harmonious and therefore energetically lighter practice space for all of us and for everyone. After a good year and a half, our participants also observed how much progress their fellow practition-ers had made, which again boosted motivation and fostered a more open and vulnerable sharing space.

However, we should also mention that some highly motivated members eventually left our small group of disciplined participants. It was simply too much of a challenge to be a regular participant. Initially, everyone agreed that only illness or death would be valid reasons to miss a session, but over time, this proved difficult for some to maintain.

I 24: Many years later, as our mediumistic development group grew to more than 14 regular participants, we became more flexible with our admission rules. Today, we meet online once a week, nearly year-round, for two hours of practice. Participants commit to attending for one month at a time. If they know in advance that vacations, business trips, hospital stays, or other commitments will prevent them from attending at least three sessions during a month, they simply skip that month and rejoin the following one. This approach helps us maintain a stable group size and allows us to focus deeply on a specific mediumistic aspect each month. New participants interested in joining may attend the first practice session of the month to experience the group dynamic and facilitation style. During this session, we also introduce the monthly topic. By the end of the month, participants often notice and enjoy their progress in mediumship.

Welcoming Participants: Earthly and Spiritual

The number of your participants depends on the size of the space available for practicing. The room should have enough space to allow pair work and small group work (groups of 3 or 4) without participants having to work back-to-back or shoulder-to-shoulder. Therefore, we recommend defining a maximum number of participants in advance. We've had good experiences by only requiring those who don't regularly attend to register via email. This allowed us to check in advance whether we had enough chairs available and to ask participants to bring their own chairs, if necessary.

Besides determining the number of participants, it's also essential to decide whether to mix beginners with more experienced participants. Working exclusively with beginners or with advanced participants offers the advantage of tailoring the experience to their skill level; for instance, detailed guidance on basic exercises may not be necessary for advanced groups. However, mixed groups allow experienced participants to work with those who may not have experience but resemble the eventual external audience (clients) they work with later. We've often found it refreshing when new people join the group and share their amazement at their own mediumistic experiences with the experienced ones.

It's beneficial to emphasize in the invitation that punctuality is expected, and that late arrivals will not be admitted. This rule has proven very helpful, especially during the initial minutes when building a shared silence in meditation. Late arrivals can disrupt this peaceful atmosphere with hurried and abrupt entrances. This strict admission rule is part of a longer tradition of British spiritualist practice circles.

However, it helps the participants if the organizers point out special events in good time before the dates that could hinder punctual arrival, e.g. open sales Sundays, markets, city festivals, public demonstrations, sporting events, etc., or also road closures, rail strikes, severe weather warnings and the like.

We also recommend encouraging participants to bring a personal journal or notebook so that they can document important experiences, insights, and lessons learned as soon as possible.

*

Before we begin our group exercises or individual sessions, it is essential to invite our spirit friends and all those spiritual helpers whom we have perceived as supportive and empowering to join us.

Each person can experiment to see what works best for them, but we've found it makes a significant energetic difference when we invite spiritual helpers from the spirit realm. The intensity of the experience and the ease with which the practice session unfolds are noticeably greater compared to sessions where the group relies solely on a daily state of consciousness. We often feel how the atmosphere in the room shifts just by speaking out our invitation to the spirit friends or reciting a prayer out load. It is not uncommon for participants to comment on the heightened energy in the room. Additionally, it reassures us, as facilitators, that we're not alone in creating this practice session or workshop, but we are part of an extended spirit team.

We always invite our personal guides and our helpers (spirit team). Depending on one's beliefs and intentions (e.g., for healing, promoting peace, finding clarity), it's also possible to invite spirit guides associated with those religious or philosophical entities such as St. Teresa of Calcutta, St. Mary of Gozo, St. Francis of Assisi, St. John the Baptist, Jesus Christ, Mother Mary, Hildegard of Bingen, Shiva, Mahakala, Ganesha, Yogananda, Babaji, Mahatma Gandhi, Allah, Fatima, Lao Tzu, or Confucius. We also sometimes call on the spirit guides of our teachers or even earthly healers whose presence is known to us. Each person can follow their own inner promptings here. Naturally, we also welcome the spirit guides of our participants and invite them to join us in generating a harmonious and inspiring practice space.

Creating Your Ritual for Spiritual Connection

Everyone eventually develops their own ritual for inviting their spiritual helpers. However, we would like to offer some initial suggestions: If you worry about encountering negative energies or harmful entities, you may want to say an invitation like the following: "For this practice, I invite the highest, purest, and brightest energies to support us in this work with clarity, mindfulness, and love. I call upon X, Y, Z (names of spiritual guides, as noted above) to help us with their wisdom and kindness."

Another invitation could be: "May all spiritual helpers who support us with healing, inner peace, and harmony on our life journey positively join us in this practice."

If healing is the focus of the exercise sequence, or if I am asked for a healing, then I, Iris, also use my private healing blessing, which I am excited to share here: "Peace be with you. May your soul grow wings and soar into the light and into eternal life."

You may also ask your spiritual helpers to grant you a personal blessing or invitation phrase. Take some time for yourself and build a presence in meditative stillness. Once you've found a deep calm within, send a thought to your higher self or, if you already have contact with them, to your spirit guide. Ask them to send you your unique blessing or invitation phrase and wait patiently to receive a response in the form of meaningful thoughts. If it doesn't come the first time, keep practicing regularly, even daily if necessary. Eventually, a message will come. However, brief or unusual it may be, don't analyze it; simply write it down without commentary. I didn't fully grasp the meaning of my healing blessing initially, even though others around me found it profoundly effective.

In our first years as facilitators for mediumistic encounters, Martin and I opened the space with this healing blessing and the invitation to our spiritual friends and teachers before participants arrived. We closed the space once the last participant had left, thanking all the spiritual beings and helpers present for their shared work. Today (2024), short intentions send to the spiritual realm is enough to feel the energy rising before the meeting starts and the energy diminishing after the practice session is finished.

Cultivating a Sacred Space for Spiritual Connection

The room should be large enough to accommodate a sitting circle for all participants. It should allow all participants to practice in groups of 2, 3 or 4 without being disturbed by their neighbors due to proximity. Beginners are often distracted when they hear bits of conversation from nearby groups, or when they perceive their energies and emotions.

Ideally, the location should be accessible by public transportation or have adequate parking. We started with a space in the middle of the city, and therefore it was definitely not a room that you'd called quiet. Here, too, external distractions and noises only seem to mainly affect beginners, who are still easily irritated by outside noise. Experienced mediums, who have learned to manage their sensitivity professionally, often do not notice and are not disturbed by external sounds.

Anyone who fears that one toilet might not be enough for more than 6 people can breathe a sigh of relief. We've had up to 15 participants with just one restroom, and everything worked out wonderfully.

There are ongoing discussions about whether to hold practice groups at home. Some worry that "negative energies" might linger after practice. We haven't had this experience. In fact, after practice sessions, the energies in our living room feel very peaceful and harmonious.

For our practice meetings, we decorate our private space a little differently than usual. We may light a few candles, place a large bouquet of flowers in the circle, or put a beautiful stone or a special crystal inside. We want to show that a special moment deserves a special space. We have also met many mediums who do not value room decor and who seem to prefer a space that is as empty as possible: the less distraction, the better. For instance, our spirit friend "Rudolph" does not need any rituals like prayer or singing. However, he enjoys candlelight, a beautiful view (which means a room that is clean), and he also appreciates it if we dress up properly.

It is important not to add additional scents, perfumes, or essential oils to the room before the meeting. Spirit friends and deceased can sometimes be identified by their scents. It is harder to perceive them this way if there are already strong fragrances present in the room.

We usually set up our existing chairs in a circle before the participants arrive. We have been advised not to use chairs and seating that are too comfortable, as otherwise there is a risk that the atmosphere will become "too cozy", and the session may take on the wrong objective (social gathering). We have also had good experiences with moving very personal and bulky furniture and objects out of the way to create a working atmosphere that is as neutral as possible.

Warm tea (e.g. ginger with lemon in winter) and still water are the drinks we provide. Our participants often bring snacks to share, so there's no need for us to provide additional refreshments. For our longer practice days, we reserve tables at a nearby restaurant that serves various options (suitable for vegans, vegetarians, and meat-eaters) and offers a quick lunch (max. 1.5 hours). We plan for at least 15 minutes before and after lunch for possible travel time, short walks, and time for conversation and reflection.

Designing Tailored Practice Exercises

In the early sessions, we adhered closely to exercises given from mediums we knew personally, following their instructions precisely. As we gained experience and deepened our connection with the spirit world, we became more flexible and moved away from others' guidelines. Since we are two facilitators, Martin usually takes over the meditation and trance part and Iris is being inspired to share exercises which are more active and experimental in nature. A possible schedule for a three-hour practice meeting might look like this:

Sample Schedule for Mediumistic Exercises:

Time in minutes	General Topic	Practice Content
20´-30´	Meditation	Sitting in one's own power; inviting spiritual helpers, forming a healing circle
Ca. 40´	1st Exercise sequence	Easy introductory exercises to warm up (sensing aura, reading cards, sharing blessings); exercises that introduce the theme of the workshop
15´	Break	Restroom break; drinking and ventilating the room
Ca. 50´	2nd Exercise sequence	Advanced and in-depth exercises on the chosen theme (e.g., trance-healing, inspirational speaking)
30´	Closing Round	Feedback and review of the experience; closing meditation; organizational matters

If you want to turn a heterogeneous, perhaps even initially anxious group into a cohesive and harmonious one, we suggest focusing on "healing" as the theme for early sessions. We have found that the level of nervousness in the room escalates as exercises progress from healing to inspirational speaking (channeling) to the readings of the deceased, with the energy in the room becoming correspondingly denser and therefore more difficult to perceive. Thus, a session focused on healing is often experienced as less stressful than one focused on communication with the deceased. Depending on the session's focus group, leaders may be prepared to adjust the manner of how to motivate the group.

When working with mixed groups (i.e., beginners and advanced participants), we assign new participants or beginners to ourselves or place
them with advanced participants who are ready to take on a mentoring
role. This setup is beneficial for both sides; experienced participants can
share their calm and insights in a strengthening and reassuring
manner, while beginners offer a way for advanced participants to test
their own skills on less experienced, potentially nervous individuals.

When being in a room and facilitating the exercises, we quickly learned
that it is helpful to first explain the whole exercise, then allow participants to form small groups, and then give step-by-step guidance in a
detailed manner; we humorously call this latter step: "for our spirit
helpers." Only then, we begin moderating the exercise step-by-step,
allowing participants to follow along. We pay attention to pauses and
often let our wording be guided by our own spirit helpers.

For online practice sessions, we adjust the structure to suit the format.
First, we explain the entire exercise upfront, providing a concise version
in the chat for participants to copy or download. After a second explanation, we invite participants to ask any open questions they may have
before starting. Once all questions are addressed, we open breakout
rooms, where participants work independently in pairs or small groups,
collecting their mediumistic practice experiences on their own. During
these sessions, we do not provide detailed guidance while they are actively working together.

During extended practice phases in an in-person setting, where
participants sit together in silence, we, as moderators, avoid speaking
but use gentle cues to regain attention when needed. A subtle clearing
of the throat or a soft sound helps to tenderly draw focus, allowing us
to calmly guide the group and gradually bring the exercise to a close.
This quiet, shared physical presence creates an atmosphere of connection and focus that is easy to maintain within the same room.

In online sessions, however, the dynamic shifts. Without the shared
physical environment, subtle sounds may go unnoticed, so we adapt by
using tools specific to the virtual setting. For instance, we might send a

gentle notification in the chat, unmute briefly to share a soft verbal cue, or use a pre-arranged signal like a visual timer or bell sound. These approaches ensure participants remain engaged while respecting the flow of the exercise.

Additionally, online sessions often require more explicit instructions beforehand, as moderators have less ability to "read the room" and intervene non-verbally. Despite the differences, our goal remains the same: to maintain a supportive, seamless transition into and out of practice phases, fostering a deep, focused experience for all participants.

Facilitating Group Dynamics and Questions

The challenges of moderating a mediumistic practice group are greater than we initially assumed. It involves answering individual participants' questions with the input of other attendees commenting on, and the participants' answers need to be commented on and corrected if necessary. Finally, it is important to move on to the final and thereby keep an eye on the time. You first need to develop a good sense of how much time individuals can be given for their statements, to ensure that individuals feel understood while avoiding lengthy digressions. It helps to sense how much resonance the responses generate within the group and to act accordingly so that a drop in attention and group energy is avoided in good time. A good indicator is to observe whether unrest is spreading in the group and whether the participants who are not affected remain present or not (eyes awake/eyes wandering into the distance).

Questions asked at the beginning of the practice session often led to time-consuming discussions that are not always effective in terms of content and focus. We therefore recommend holding a "question-and - answer session" after the initial meditation, ideally at the end of our event (please allow time for this). Then the participants are usually more centered, filled with new experiences that can only be verbalized to a limited extent, and more reflective and open to the answers of others. In the answers we give, we always make it clear that we are answering according to our current level of knowledge and mediumistic experience, but that we are not professional (neither medium nor psychic) in this field. When responding to other participants, we intend to answer in a positive, constructive and respectful attitude and to communicate in appreciative manner.

It is always helpful for facilitators, especially in disharmonious moments, to remember that all participants gathered in the practice room have been led to this practice session by their spiritual helpers. The participants are present because they have a role in radiating their light further. Every single one of them is essential to bring healing, peace, love, and divine truth into the world for the benefit of all people. But this also means that our spiritual friends know for whom we are the right practitioners and for whom we are not. This view has given us self-assurance, even in moments when we have been led to our own inner limits of patience and understanding.

Facilitating Reflective Feedback

The timing for providing mutual feedback on the exercises can vary depending on the objective:

1. *immediately after the first praxis round, i.e., after Participant 1 has been active, but Participant 2 was not yet active,*

2. *or after all practice sequences have been completed, i.e., after all participants have been active.*

The shorter the time interval between feedback and practice sequences, the better participants can recall their experiences made. The disadvantage, however, is that the energy built up from the exercise is dissipated again through talking and the rationalization or doubts that often accompany it. This immediate feedback may lead to a perception of brief energetic interruption.

We have found it very enriching when we have created exercise sequences in which there has been no verbal feedback about what has happened over a long period of time, sometimes even for the entire time. Here, we practiced unconditional service with our practice partners. We then noticed a greater presence of the participants in the perception of their own mediumistic experiences. To document their own progress and record the feedback results, it is helpful for participants to bring a media diary in which they can write down and record their experiences and insights.

Insights and Inspirations from Our Journey

I: When Gordon and the participants asked us to lead a mediumistic practice group in the Frankfurt area, I initially resisted. At the time, my professional schedule was so full of appointments that I had no idea when we should have done it. Besides, we were still beginners in our first year and had no idea about our mediumistic abilities. It took a few months before we made our first attempt, and something wonderful happened: not only did my calendar magically arrange itself so that I could regularly co-lead the practice groups during the week. There were also enough participants so that the meetings could take place regularly.

The wonderful thing was that from the very beginning, we both felt guided during the moderation of these practice groups. We were able to give spontaneous answers to questions that we had not previously been aware of. However, these answers were confirmed as coherent in our supervision by Matthew Smith.

M: Later, many months later, I spontaneously led a morning meditation at a workshop, while the participants were waiting for Steven Levett, who was delayed due to traffic issues. As the course supervisor, I gave the participants a choice: they could either spend the time chatting and waiting, or they could start preparing for the seminar. When they chose the latter, the only remaining question was who should lead the meditation. When the choice fell on me, I simply began with my starting meditation "Sit down and do nothing!", inspired by the early instructions of one of my teachers, Grandmaster Zhi Chang Li. When Steven Levett finally arrived, visibly stressed and flustered, the whole group was already in the middle of the meditation. Steven gestured for me to continue and finish the exercise before he took over.

The tension I experienced while leading the meditation, hopefully, wasn't too noticeable to the participants. Yes, I had led meditations before, but so far in small circles and often with the help of notes I'd compiled from various meditations by Gordon for my own use. Now, here I was, speaking freely in front of a group of 50 participants –it was a different ball game for me. Trusting that the spirit world would provide the necessary support, I spoke and surprised myself with the stringency and clarity of my instructions.

Months later, in a middle of a regular weekend seminar, Gordon Smith asked me to lead the morning meditation in his presence and in my native German language. He also added that he trusted us –Iris and me– as teachers, mediums, and friends. That was truly a "accolade" moment. From that point on, there was no turning back. Deeply touched, but also tense, I recognized that it was indeed my task to lead practice circles together with Iris. It was time to embrace this responsibility and grow through the shared experience. I started to offer meditation and mediumistic exercise evenings (practice groups) through the Frankfurter Ring e.V. – at the beginning physically at the Frankfurt Youth Hostel, where, years ago, I had my first "critical" encounter with Gordon Smith.

Chapter V:

Frequently Asked Questions

The love for the deceased and the love for what we call "eternal light" form the foundation of all communication. Based on this simple insight, we would like to answer some central questions we have collected for you:

Why is it so difficult to communicate with the deceased? Isn't there an easier, simpler way?

Indeed, at the beginning, it seems difficult or even impossible to establish a stable connection with the spirit world. This is because both sides are not entirely sure how it works, or they are not yet well attuned to each other. Fundamentally, it becomes quite simple once access has been established, and trust on the human side is so strong that doubts, fantasies, and self-deception do not enter the communication.

The difficulty also lies in the fact that no one can explain exactly how it works. It's like trying to explain to someone how best to ride a bike. It sounds simple in theory, but only practice shows to what extent the individual is able to get in tune with the bike so that they can get around on it. However, once you have learned how to ride a bike, it is very easy. This doesn't mean there won't be days when biking doesn't go so smoothly, or that there aren't stretches of road that cause you to stumble. But basically, you know how it works. And it's the same with swimming or preparing a good meal.

I am not sure if I am imagining all of this, or if I am truly communicating with a being from the spirit world. How can I tell the difference?

In the beginning, it is indeed not easy to distinguish the difference. Often, one feels genuinely connected to the spirit world, only because of a strong expectation within oneself. It may therefore be unclear. You will notice the difference whenever you receive images or messages that you could never have thought of yourself. Or when they are accompanied by such a profound feeling of peace, love, and inner certainty that you know clearly that you really did not create this content yourself.

On your mediumistic journey, you gradually begin to gather experiences. As you reflect on each exercise and compare your perceptions, you'll start to discern the differences between the distinct qualities of communication—receiving messages from the spirit world—and what originates from your own imagination. Both have their purpose, as we, your spirit guides, only truly work with your imagination and creative ability when you are connected with us in trust. Before that, we use your imagination and fantasy to teach you the difference between worldly and transcendent nature playfully.

I: In the beginning, I didn't believe that people who are very critical, skeptical or very fearful could influence me in my mediumistic work. But it is true for those starting on this mediumistic journey: if the recipient of a message does not radiate trust, the connection between the being in the spiritual world, the medium and the recipient cannot flow with the full energy of love and "message conductivity". This is different with a recipient who is ready to receive a message from the Other World full of confidence and inner peace. So even the greatest effort on our part sometimes has little influence on the "message conductivity" of the medium.

I find it difficult to practice regularly. Can I still make progress?

Although it's especially helpful in the beginning to complete the exercises in a disciplined and designated sequence, we utilize every attempt you make to advance you on your spiritual path. No effort, no matter how small, remains without an echo. As long as your intention is clear and pure, and you're willing to overcome difficulties on your spiritual journey, you will always receive the support you need.

It's also entirely possible that you become familiar with mediumship at a stage in life when a deeper engagement may not be feasible or even desirable. The love for your family members, as well as your duties and tasks of daily life, are just as much a part of your spiritual growth as the mediumistic practice times. Each of you has your own pace, own rhythm, and own condition and therefor your own discipline on which we build. And you can be assured that we know you well —and possibly even better than you know yourselves; only then is a strong and deep connection with you possible.

Is it possible that negative or even evil spirits could influence me on my path through mediumship?

As long as you use your mediumship to serve others with love, trust, and clarity, you need not worry that you will be led astray; you have nothing bad to fear. You will find that in your connection with us, you will experience a heavenly sense of certainty, inner peace, and a state of consciousness that is difficult or even impossible to achieve in everyday life. Love is the foundation, and it is true.

All other entities, such as evil spirits, demons, or underworld figures, stem from human imagination, which is primarily based on fear. Fear cannot exist where love is present; and one of the experiences you will have is, that you are full of love. There is no room for fear unless you paint fear against the wall and focus your attention on it. The darkness cannot swallow the light, because where there is light, there is no more darkness. The light excludes the darkness.

Such is the relationship between love and fear: you are in a state of love the moment you are full of trust, feel peace, and reside fully in your presence. You can reach this state through mediumship, among other paths, as this state of love is the channel that connects you with all the dear beings from the Other World. Love will help you to grow beyond yourselves, if you want to.

Your imagination creates the spirits of fear, the demons of dread, hatred, and despair. It is not the forces of the spirit world that create demons, but rather you yourselves. So, you can choose whether you want to be influenced by your own negative thoughts or not. But don't let yourself be intimidated by your own imagination and power of thought: you are full of love, and you are light, that continues to expand the longer you exist.

I: My spirit guides repeatedly emphasize in their messages that we are protected, and that negative thoughts or evil spirits cannot harm us unless we consciously decide to do so. One of my training partners was even told by her spirit guide that dark or malevolent spirits could not even come near her, if they existed at all. This was because she was surrounded by many loving deceased people who together —and with all their love and care for her— formed a large sphere of light and love around her, so that no unauthorized access to her would be possible at all.

If you believe in the existence of evil forces, the idea that departed souls stand by us protectively, caringly, and lovingly can offer great comfort. My experiences over the years have shown me that far more caring and supportive souls are by my side than I ever imagined. My teachers have assured me that this is true for anyone who lives constructively and with a spiritual focus.

What can I do with my mediumistic abilities?

This depends on the direction in which your personal path unfolds. The exercises presented here will help you to independently develop the foundation that are necessary to be able to communicate with us, the spirit world, as a pure channel. As mentioned at the beginning, these skills can also be acquired in other ways. But we want to create the opportunity for anyone who wants to, to consciously take the mediumistic path and make successful
progress.

The goal of our practice session is not only to strengthen your spiritual being, but also to enhance your self-love and your own trust. Beyond that, we want to lead you to greater inner clarity and enable you to connect with us, the spiritual beings, at any time.

Once this connection is established, we will take over your further training by giving you impulses and insights. We will also guide you into specific life situations allowing you to further develop and nurture your spiritual competencies. In the initial stage, we focus on your personal growth, later you will test and experience your mediumistic skills in collaboration with others.

This only happens if you want it yourself. There are many who only use their mediumistic ability quietly, for themselves and for their personal path. That is more than we could hope for.

Of course, you may also dream of one day becoming a professional medium available to others. But for many of you, this is a long and challenging path that requires much discipline and sincerity in practice. Becoming a medium is a goal that cannot be immediately set, but should be pursued only after many months, if not years.

We recommend not dedicating yourself to this calling right away but initially focusing on applying your abilities in everyday life, practicing the exercises, and building trust and love. These are steps on your journey that demand much of your time and attention. Be mindful of this and take your time. Many things need to be explored, and many of your (sometimes presumed) mediumistic gifts will be tested and examined in daily life.

I: I remember Gordon Smith mentioning at the very beginning of our first training that it usually takes decades to become a professional medium. He advised us to anticipate at least seven years. Reflecting on my own path, I would agree with him. As has been repeatedly emphasized, this journey is not just about acquiring mediumistic skills but strengthening your own personal maturity. For me, everyday life events shaped me during this period just as much as the weekly mediumistic practice sessions I committed to.

We would also like to share the following observation in recent years: Some participants tend to pursue the mediumistic path more closely when they feel a sense of emptiness in their lives. They try to resolve their existential crises through mediumship, which is not necessarily effective. If there is a significant inner need, this must first be fulfilled through personal growth. One's spiritual abilities will later develop genuinely on a foundation of unconditional readiness to serve.

Can I make mistakes on my mediumistic path?

No, that is not possible, because experiences you collect are necessary for your own growth. As long as you practice alone and follow the exercises in the given order, nothing can happen that cannot be turned into a positive spiritual experience. If you feel uncertain, ask your spirit guides to help you at that moment; they are always willing to assist.

Even if you believe you are not yet in contact with them, they will help you take the next step. They do so with joy and dedication, surrounding you with a love far beyond what you can experience on earth. Even if you do not feel this, it happens continuously at every stage of your spiritual journey. So, trust in them and allow them to be your teachers.

Will pursuing the mediumistic path cause me to lose my sense of grounding or disconnect me from reality?

Well, that depends a bit on you, but ultimately, it's similar to any other discipline. If you devote yourself exclusively to one topic in life, you might become dependent or even addicted to it, leading to an unbalanced and unfulfilling life. We suggest viewing the development of your own mediumistic path like learning a new language. If you spend the entire day practicing vocabulary and cramming grammar but neglect physical activity, your muscles will become stiff, and one day, you may find yourself not quite as fit as you were at the start. Additionally, if you stop tending to the financial foundations of your life —namely, your daily work— you'll soon find yourself struggling to make ends meet.

Of course, there are talented interpreters who have made translation their profession and live off it. But they are the minority; there are tens of thousands of people who learn a new language to bring joy to themselves and those close to them, helping to overcome misunderstandings due to existing language barriers. They use their acquired skill to foster peace in this world. It's similar with mediumship: it won't provide you with everything you need to stay physically healthy or maintain financial stabile.

Those among you who hope to form friendships with beings from the spirit world because they find it difficult to make friends among their fellow humans and feel lonely will also be disappointed. Earthly laws apply to you just as they do to everyone else, and that includes connecting with people of your kind. Therefore, we recommend that those affected confront this aspect of physical reality, with all its advantages and disadvantages first.

What happens to me when I transition to the Other World? What happens to my deceased soul?

This is a challenging question that can be answered differently depending on one's worldview and level of development. One thing is certain: you will continue to exist as a soul even after you have left your physical body.

However, the form this takes depends on what your soul has defined for itself as a field of development or growth after the transition. The love you feel for family members, friends, animals, and even plants make it possible for you to connect and undertake the journey together.

The world on your side is bound by space and time, but the beyond is multidimensional, offering not just one possibility but countless others. If, however, you communicate with your spirit guides or even your departed loved ones, know that they connect with you in a form that will resonate with you.

Unfortunately, everything we convey to you about the other world is only a makeshift explanation for what truly awaits you there. For this reason, we recommend choosing a concept of what happens after death that provides you with the greatest support and reassurance for life in your world. Look closely at whether your idea of the afterlife instills fear or trust, whether it holds you back from fully enjoying life here in all its aspects. Reject all concepts that demotivate you, diminish your greatness, and prevent you from being your true self.

How do I recognize a good mediumistic teacher? Whom should I turn to for deeper learning?

The exercises in this book are designed to help you learn to distinguish when information comes from your imagination and when it originates from the spirit world. Once the connection is established, you will be guided to your (next) teachers. This guidance may come in the form of a gut feeling, a constant reference to a particular seminar or event, or simply a yearning to get to know a certain mediumistic teacher better.

Again, the principle applies: the teacher should create a space where you can develop with trust and without fear. Mediumship cannot be learned through strictness or ambition. Mediumship unfolds in its own time, and a suitable teacher for you has not only the necessary patience but also the ability to provide the right guidance at the right moment. Trust your intuition if the connection is not yet established and be open to encountering teachers who may try to instruct you but may not facilitate your growth.

Your earthly teachers have the task of enriching you with new experiences, knowledge transfer, and inspiration. They connect you with your true teachers, who are not found outside of you but within. Thus, building trust with your own spirit guides and deceased relatives is the foundation upon which your personal development rests. And once you have learned to read this inner compass with trust and without misinterpretation, you are ready to be lovingly taught and guided by your true teachers.

These teachers often know you better than you know yourself; they perceive you without judgment and bring infinite patience to help you, often in various ways, experience and learn what will best support you in developing and unfolding your mediumship at that moment.

This may, at times, lead to a dissonance between what an earthly teacher explains and believes to be true and what you yourself receive as truth within. In such cases, you will have to decide, and you may need to revisit this decision by asking yourself: Who do I trust more: the earthly teacher or my own inner teacher, or the teaching team from the spirit world?

I: In my own development, there were several occasions to take this 'trust test. It's not only about following what feels right and truthful within but also about continuing to meet the earthly "teacher" with trust and openness. Everything that is brought to us, whether from the earthly or spirit world, is simply an impulse or suggestion. It is up to us to responsibly decide whether to gratefully take these suggestions or to leave them as they are: well-intended impulses and hints. Responsibility for our own development always lies with us, and it is not assumed by the spirit world.

Chapter VI:
Spirit Guide Teachings

It has been truly wonderful, genuine, and profoundly enriching for us to engage with these texts and exercises for our mediumistic growth. We are filled with gratitude, humility, and immense joy for the opportunity to undertake this translation from one worldly language to another over the past few days. Yet, time and again, the desire arose to let our dear spirit friend "Rudolph" share his perspective with you directly. Thus, this additional chapter was born, featuring quotations from our German book: "Nachrichten aus der Anderen Welt, Band 1" (Messages from the Other World, Volume 1-5).

These books collecting the literal transcription of all the conversations we had with "Rudolph" during the first months of our connection. Even in the early stages, we received valuable insights into the unfolding of our own spirituality and mediumship. While the unique melody and rhythm of "Rudolph's" characteristic language may have been some-what diminished through the process of translation, we hope the follow-ing content will still inspire and guide you on your own spiritual journey:

*

On September 27th, 2019: It fills us with joy to feel how deeply con-nected you are with us and to sense your devotion to maintaining this bond. Know this: it is your dedication that allows us to strengthen our connection with you and to make our presence known. Rest assured; we are always here. Even if it doesn't always feel that way to you, the cause lies solely within you. When you are rooted in love, devotion, and alignment with yourself, you can sense us; you can feel our ever-present nearness.

In our realm, everything is one —a single, unified thought. Whenever a fragment of this thought separates itself, it is drawn, as if by a powerful magnet, to the energy source that is open and receptive at that moment. This is what matters most to us: sensing that there are humans, animals, beings, and energies seeking contact with us. When that call comes, we respond.

Do not be alarmed if I am not always the presence you expect to be at your side. When I feel your inquiry, I find a way for you to recognize me. In fact, I had considered appearing to you as a small dog during our first encounters. But that is not something you need.

*

On September 30th, 2019: You are not meant to share your experiences through many words. It is actions that matter. Your radiant presence in the world, just as it is, is the only important act you need to fulfill. The desire to stand at the forefront or to lead a group does not genuinely aid in spreading the light. It is simply about being — being connected, lovingly and wholeheartedly. And it is not about expecting a response to your actions. Instead, it is about letting what we pass on to you through our connection flow with humility, calmness, and serenity.

Trust that the bond between us and you is always woven with love, for it is love alone that forms this connection. Love is the only word in your language that comes close to expressing what we are.

*

On October 4th, 2019: We are often asked why we seek contact with you and why we maintain this connection. The answer is very simple: you and we, you and I, are one. There is no separation, and we are always connected, so it is the most natural thing for us to communicate with one another. There is no separation.

We —I, we— are always and everywhere present, though in a form that your human senses cannot directly perceive. For this reason, all the machines and devices developed so far —yes, I'm speaking about technology— are unable to capture or manifest us, unless we choose to make it so. And how much more beautiful it is to be perceived by a loving human being and to exchange through the simplest form of communication. You already know how close we are to you. And you know that no technical device is needed to perceive us.

We are simply here.

And the further away you search for us, using techniques that go beyond the limits of human perception, the further you distance yourselves from us. We don't need a recording device, a phonograph, or any apparatus to capture us photographically. The reason is simple:

Because we are already here.

Your senses, the ones you naturally posses, are more than enough. When paired with the desire for connection and the bond that unites us, these senses are all you need to be with us. Truly, each moment of this connection is a celebration, if you look at it that way.

*

On October 23rd, 2019: I sense a certain excitement. Could that be? So often, we struggle to differentiate between joy and tension. The sensations feel remarkably similar. Both create an elevated state: one with a positive connotation, the other with a negative one. And yet, these are the vibrations that make it easier for us to establish a connection with you.

This is why it's often easier when Martin is tired, stressed, or joyful. But joy —true joy— is the easiest way to open the channel between us. Joy is a unique treasure, whether it springs from something small or something profoundly moving. The distinction doesn't really matter, as it can be challenging to recognize, in the present moment, whether something is truly significant. Time often reveals that what felt weighty was ordinary, while what seemed trivial was, in fact, essential. This means that pure joy — unconditional joy— is what allows you to grow personally.

*

On October 14, 2019: Please don't be startled if we announce our presence with signals like cracking or knocking before we appear. These are simply shifts in the atmosphere, changes that the matter around you absorbs and reflects. You might also notice shadows flickering in your field of vision, sudden shifts in color, or even the sensation of a light breeze. All of these can arise as subtle signs of our imminent presence.

Do not fear these moments. They are merely heralds, gentle signals meant to help you prepare for what is coming or even to anticipate it with joy. For us, it is pure joy that fills the space whenever we reconnect with you.

*

On October 26th, 2019: Take care of yourself and your inner energy balance so striving to remain as centered as possible, like a closed system. It's easy to fall into the trap of giving too much to others or expecting too much in return. However, trusting that enough will naturally flow and understanding that you are not the sole source of giving for everyone on this earth can bring a sense of peace. Knowing that self-responsibility lies not only with ourselves but also with others can help you navigate daily life more smoothly.

I have always been aware —though I have not always acted accordingly— that I am personally responsible for myself. However, whenever I did take responsibility for myself and my actions, my inner balance was restored.

On November 9th, 2019: The transition from life to the Other Life happens, in human terms, within mere fractions of a second. Once this transition is complete, the memory of earthly life is initially forgotten. The passage of the individual soul into the collective, into the All-Oneness —far more intricate, complete, and authentic than anything on earth— occurs instantly. From that moment, the concept of time ceases to exist.

Yet, when individuals reach out with love, seeking connection and sending their heartfelt desire for closeness to the spirit world — to us— soul groups are reactivated. This allows what was once felt on earth to be experienced again in direct connection.

By setting the intention and expressing the desire for contact, earthly faculties are reawakened, as if drawn by a magnet. The soul is then able to establish —or reestablish— the connection. In that moment, communication becomes possible. The soul is always integrated within the All-Oneness. Yet, to honor the heartfelt wish of the one reaching out, it extends its hand, joyfully fulfilling the desire for connection.

*

December 8th, 2019: Why do I appear to you as the person I do? Why not someone else, someone who was more significant in the world? Why is it me?

We respond to the intention you set, presenting ourselves in a form you can understand: in a language that the medium can express, with words and images that resonate within the shared universe of you and the medium. Idle chatter would be pointless and would simply waste resources. We choose a form of communication that is comprehensible to you, building trust —at least in the beginning. It would make little sense for Mother Mary, speaking Aramaic, to seek contact with you. How could you verify that it is truly her responding to your questions and addressing your wishes?

We draw upon the knowledge and context of those who seek us. Communicating in a language foreign to you or the medium would be a waste of energy. While the effect might be there, the resonance would be hollow. Building trust is the foundation of what we do. We are neither magicians nor illusionists. We work with what is available and give you the opportunity to verify our presence. Only then can genuine communication take place. Appearing as Cleopatra or Caesar would not even be entertaining — it would simply be futile and wasted effort. Instead, appearing as a physicist, whose life and biography can be researched and validated, ensures that nothing meaningless is conveyed.

Over time, it is possible —and likely— that the way we interact will evolve. For now, however, the three of us function like a finely tuned apparatus in my workshop: a divergent beam of light passes through a system of lenses, projecting an image onto a screen.

*

May 5th, 2020: Iris: I would like to ask a follow-up question, focusing on the trance state Martin is currently in: Do you require or draw upon any earthly energies to make this possible? And how is it that he emerges from the trance feeling strengthened, while our usual daily activities often leave us utterly exhausted? What exactly happens in this process?

Nothing happens, and that is the source of our connection. Unconditional being gives rise to unconditional energy, opening the way for support both emotionally and physically. It is only through the fact that no physical energy is withdrawn that it becomes comprehensible in this, your world, that recovery can occur. If the process of transmission were one that absorbed energy, then a medium would awaken exhausted, seeking help and needing time, speaking of headaches and piercing sensations, and wanting to take distance; but no. Nothingness, calmness, and the open channel are the answers to this question.

August 16th, 2020: When people come together in the same spirit to bring about healing, to send healing, or when they embark on pilgrimages, traveling long distances to reach a specific place and meet others who share the same spirit, they are ultimately doing this for themselves. They seek to perceive and recognize themselves, to see reflections of their own being in the radiant faces of others. This is because they cannot bear that the people who surround them in their daily lives often lack that same radiance— something they so deeply long to see.

Thus, gathering with like-minded individuals provide support for each person, and the collective energy of the group amplifies this strength. Yet, it is important to remember: true connection is not something we need to create, for we are already connected. Nevertheless, these gatherings strengthen our ability to navigate daily life, to live on Earth during the time we are here.

Still, it's essential to reflect on the following:

- To what extent do I distance myself from my true self when I grant another more strength than I give myself?

- Why should I trust someone else more than I trust myself?

- Why should I honor someone else before first honoring myself?

- Why should I put myself second to others?

- Why compare?

Always remember, when you are with a group of people, to remain centered in yourself, to stay in your own balance, living and being in your core even as you connect with others. The highest form of this kind of togetherness is sitting in silence —feeling the connection in this small circle— and then dissolving the circle again.

Even so, exercises are important, whether one-on-one or in a group, as they help you become aware of yourself and allow you to exchange experiences. Through this exchange, you can discover what the other person has experienced, provided their words truly reflect what was felt. But please, always take care never to diminish yourself in comparison to another.

Epilogue

At the end of this book, we congratulate you on embarking upon this journey with us. Even if not every exercise brought about what you thought you wanted to experience, you can now be confident that every single step has brought you a little closer to your mediumistic side of life.

Even more important than this is that you have been given the confidence and the knowledge that there is more than what you thought you knew. Now, you have gained access to a source of love, insight, and peace, which can be helpful and useful in your everyday life if you want it to be.

You have learned to use the compass of love and to practice your own mediumistic path with dedication. Looking back, you will find that much has changed in your life and that you have gathered experiences you might not have thought possible at the beginning of your journey.

Now, we let you go with love and look forward to accompanying you on each of your next steps, whether mediumistic or otherwise.

With deep love,

Your spirit friends

Attachments

Inspirational Reads: A Selection of Favorites

Harry Boddington (1995) "The university of spiritualism", Psychic Press LT. The Coach House

Harry Edwards (1996/2012) "A guide for the development of mediumship", Con-PSY Publications

Eileen Garret (2016) "Her Life and Her Mediumship", SDU Publication

Helen Greaves (1969) Testimony of light: An extraordinary message of life after death, Rider

Estelle Roberts (2010) "Fifty Years a Medium", SDU Publications

Gordon Smith (2010) "How to Become a Medium", Allegria Taschenbuch

Gordon Smith (2018)"Mediumship Made Easy", Hay House UK

Gordon Smith (2018) "Beyond Reasonable Doubt", Coronet UK

Matthew Smith (2001) "Entrancement: A Theoretical and Practical Manuel", Spirits Publications

Ramadahn Trust (various); "Truth in the Spirit world: In lecture of Ramadahn through the Medium of Ursula Roberts", Volume 1-7

Silver Birch Series (various, e.g.1938) by A.W. Austun. "Teachings of Silver Birch", Spiritual Truth Press

If you speak German, you might be interested in one of our books:

Iris & Martin Magin (2023) „Medialität Jetzt 2.0. Dein medialer Wegweiser", BoD

Iris & Martin Magin (2020) „Nachrichten aus der Anderen Welt

(Band 1), BoD

The Language of Mediumship: Terms for Beginners

When we first published the German version of this book, we lacked a comprehensive understanding of the common terminology used in spirit communication, both in German and English. Six years later, we are more aware that certain terms in the English-speaking world carry specific connotations that we initially used somewhat blindly. Some of these terms have no direct equivalent in German, and we often found ourselves guessing their intended meaning.

To help non-native speakers navigate similar challenges, we have compiled a brief overview of frequently used terms and their meanings. This glossary is based on AI-supported research and may not always align perfectly with culturally specific interpretations. However, it serves as a helpful starting point for non-native speakers engaging with English-speaking environments in the context of spirit communication.

Common Spiritual Terms and their Key Features

Term	Definition	Key Features	Involves Spirits?
Medi-umistic	Abilities involving communication with the spirit world, specifically with spirits of the deceased.	Requires a direct connection to the spirit realm; distinct from psychic abilities but often overlaps.	*Yes*
Me-dium-ship	The structured practice of serving as an intermediary between the living and the spirit world.	Includes evidence-based communication (validating details about spirits); follows ethical guidelines.	*Yes*

Term	Definition	Key Features	Involves Spirits?
Higher Self	The aspect of an individual's consciousness deeply connected to universal wisdom or divine knowledge.	Often accessed through meditation or introspection; acts as a bridge between the physical self and the spiritual realm.	No
Spirit Guide	A specific spirit assigned to guide, support, and provide wisdom to an individual throughout life.	A singular or small group of spirits guiding the individual, offers personal guidance and protection, often associated with a specific purpose	Yes
Spirit Beings	A general term for entities existing in the non-physical realms, not limited to guides.	Broad category, may include ancestors, deities and other non-human entities, vary in roles	Yes
Spirit World	The realm or dimension where spirits exist after physical death.	Often associated with afterlife; Focused on spirits of deceased beings; Place of connection	Yes
Spiritual World	A broader concept of the non-material realms encompassing all spiritual dimensions and energies.	Includes all spiritual aspects beyond just spirits; involves divine, energetic, and broader metaphysical phenomena.	Yes

Term	Definition	Key Features	Involves Spirits?
Philo-sophical Commu-nication	Spirit communi-cation that con-veys profound spiritual teach-ings or universal truths.	Focuses on universal truths, spiritual laws, or insights; often comes from higher beings or ascended masters.	*Yes*
Spirit Commu-nication	The general practice of con-necting with spirits, whether they are loved ones, guides, or entities.	Includes both direct (through a medium) and indirect (through intuition or signs) interactions.	*Yes*
Channel-ing	Allowing a spir-itual entity or higher con-sciousness to communicate through the channeler.	Involves light or deep trance states; may in-clude spoken, writ-ten, or artistic ex-pressions of mes-sages.	*Yes*
Auto-matic Writing	A form of chan-neling where messages are received from spirits or higher beings and writ-ten uncon-sciously.	The individual allows their hand to move freely, guided by spiritual influence; often used for per-sonal or philosophi-cal messages.	*Yes*

Term	Definition	Key Features	Involves Spirits?
Telepathy	The ability to transmit or receive thoughts, feelings, or mental impressions without using the five physical senses.	Often associated with deep energetic connections between individuals; can occur between living beings or spiritual entities.	*Sometimes*
Astral Projection	The conscious experience of leaving one's physical body to explore the spiritual or astral planes.	Often intentional, achieved through meditation or trance states; involves a sense of awareness outside the physical form.	*Sometimes*
Intuitive Readings	A form of insight or guidance drawn from heightened intuition or inner knowing.	Focuses on inner knowing rather than external entities; often interprets energy, emotions, or life patterns.	*No*
Psychic Readings	A person with extrasensory perception (ESP) to read energy, people, or situations beyond the senses.	May include perceiving past, present, or future events (precognition, clairvoyance); focuses on energy fields.	*No*

Term	Definition	Key Features
Clairvoy-ance	The ability to see visions, images, or symbols in the mind's eye that provide insight or messages.	Often associated with psychic abilities. Can involve glimpses of past, present, or future events.
Clairaudi-ence	The ability to hear messages, sounds, or voices from the spiritual realm or through heightened intuition.	Can be internal (in the mind) or external (audible to the ear). Commonly used in mediumship or spirit communication.
Claircogni-zance	A sudden inner knowing or awareness of information without logical explanation, often intuitive downloads.	Involves clear and immediate understanding, without external input. Frequently associated with intuitive or psychic practices.
Clairal-ience	The ability to perceive smells from the spiritual or energetic realm, often tied to spirit communication.	Can involve smelling fragrances, odors, or familiar scents linked to spirits or energy. Less common than other "clair" abilities.

Summary

The topic of mediumship, especially in the concrete form of communication with the deceased, evokes fear among many German-speaking individuals and sparks more skepticism and doubt than it deserves. In this book, the authors, with the support of their spirit team, have taken the bold step of offering curious readers simple exercises to help them experience their first mediumistic encounters.

The authors aim not only to convey initial skills also to work out the underlying criteria for success. Through their own practical experiences, they demonstrate that the mediumistic path is accessible to anyone —even to those who have not yet recognized any inherent mediumistic gifts.

At the heart of this book are 12 practice units that allow for a self-directed mediumistic study without prior knowledge. These exercises are simple, clear, and practical. Apart from a little time, only require the courage to embark on a mediumistic adventure. By the end of this series of exercises, readers will be able to establish a lasting connection with their own spiritual helpers and maintain this contact —as if using a "mediumistic telephone"— with confidence.

The individual exercises are dedicated, among other things, to providing the necessary mediumistic energies, dissolving emotional, physical and mental blocks and offering initial self-healing techniques.

Iris received these texts over approximately four weeks while practicing trance writing during a summer vacation. From the beginning, Iris's spiritual friends were actively involved in creating this book. The introductory texts and 12 exercises are supplemented by testimonials from Iris and Martin. The appeal of this book lies in capturing the perspectives of two distinctly practicing mediums. They complement the exercises transmitted from the spirit world, showing readers that one does not have to be born a medium to embark on a successful mediumistic journey.

Acknowledgments

We would like to extend our heartfelt gratitude to all the mediumistic teachers and spiritual lecturers who have profoundly enriched our journey, both in personal encounters and during events hosted by institutions such as the Frankfurter Ring e.V. (Frankfurt/Main, Germany) and the Arthur Findlay College (Stansted, UK). In particular, we are deeply grateful to Gordon Smith and Matthew Smith for their inspiring guidance and mentorship, which provided a strong foundation for our initial steps into the world of mediumship.

We also wish to express our sincere thanks to the developers of AI technology. Their innovative tools enabled us to translate this book in record time and refine it into the version you now hold in your hands.

Finally, we offer our deepest appreciation to our friend "Rudolph," whose presence and wisdom were instrumental in bringing this work into being.